Design and Launch an Online
E-Commerce Business

Other Titles in the Click Start Series

Design and Launch an Online Boutique Business in a Week

Design and Launch an Online Gift Business in a Week

Design and Launch an Online Travel Business in a Week

Design and Launch an Online Networking Business in a Week

Entrepreneur MAGAZINE'S
CLICKSTARTS

Design and Launch an Online

E-Commerce Business

in a WEEK

◆ *Build a Retail Site in Just One Week*

◆ *Programming Skills and Design Knowledge Not Required*

◆ *Discover Inexpensive Solutions from Yahoo, GoDaddy, Google and eBay*

Entrepreneur Press & Jason R. Rich

EP
Entrepreneur.
Press

Jere L. Calmes, Publisher
Cover Design: Desktop Miracles
Production and Composition: Eliot House Productions

This publication is designed to provide accurate and authoritative information in regard to the subject matter covered. It is sold with the understanding that the publisher is not engaged in rendering legal, accounting or other professional services. If legal advice or other expert assistance is required, the services of a competent professional person should be sought.

Computer icon ©Skocko
Hand icon ©newyear2008

Library of Congress Cataloging-in-Publication Data

    Design and launch an ecommerce business in a week/by Entrepreneur Press and Jason R. Rich.

       p.   cm. —(Click start series)

    ISBN-13: 978-1-59918-183-7 (alk. paper)

    ISBN-10: 1-59918-183-5

       1. Electronic commerce. 2. New business enterprises—Computer networks. I. Rich, Jason. II. Entrepreneur Press.

    HF5548.32.D475 2008

    658.8'72—dc22   2008015782

Printed in Canada

13 12 11 10 09 08   10 9 8 7 6 5 4 3 2 1

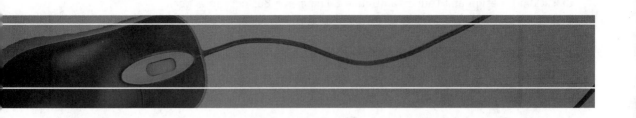

Contents

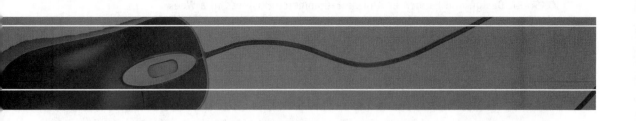

Acknowledgments

*T*hanks to Jere Calmes, Courtney Thurman, and Ronald Young at Entrepreneur Press for inviting me to work on this project. This book is also possible because of the fine editing and design work of Karen Billipp and everyone at Eliot House Productions.

My never-ending love and gratitude goes out to my lifelong friends—Mark, Ellen (as well as Ellen's family), and Ferras (www.FerrasMusic.com)—who are all extremely important people in my life, as well as to my other close friends—Garrick Procter, Christopher Henry, and Chris Coates.

I'd also like to thank my family for all of their support and give a shout-out to my Yorkshire terrier "Rusty" (www.MyPalRusty.com). Yes, he has his own website, so please check it out! To visit my website, point your web browser to www.JasonRich.com.

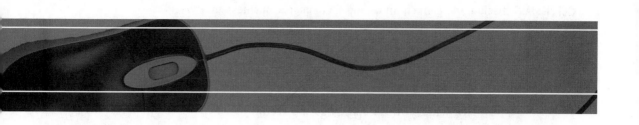

Preface

So, you've heard the hype about how ordinary people—just like you—are earning hundreds, thousands, and even millions of dollars in extra income by launching their own online businesses, often from their homes. Now, you want in on the action! Well, if you have an idea for an awesome product to sell, this book will help you get started quickly, and with the lowest initial investment possible. Best of all, no previous business experience is necessary, and you don't need to know anything about computer programming, thanks to the many *e-commerce turnkey solutions* currently available to online merchants.

Some of what you'll need to get started is:

➡ A great business idea (including ideas about what you'll be selling online and to whom)

➡ Initial investment capital to create and launch your website and to market your website for basic business supplies and for product inventory

➡ A computer with access to the internet (preferably a high-speed DSL, FIOS, or Broadband connection)

➡ Access to an e-commerce turnkey solution or website design software

➡ A willingness to work hard to get your business started

It's important to understand that *Design and Launch Your E-Commerce Website in One Week* is **not** about get-rich-quick schemes. What this book focuses on is how to sell products (as opposed to information or services) online using an e-commerce website (complete with *shopping cart* module) that you'll create, operate, and manage.

The information in this book will help you start selling virtually any product quickly and profitably, and it will help you properly identify your target

E-COMMERCE = BIG BUCKS FOR SAVVY BUSINESS OPERATORS

Revenues generated by online businesses and the online parts of traditional retail businesses during 2006 generated over $96 billion, up from $83 billion in 2004. According to the U.S. Census Bureau, "Rapid growth in e-retail has been the norm. From 2000 to 2005, retail e-sales increased at an average annual growth rate of 27.3 percent, compared with 4.3 percent for total retail sales."

The U.S. Census Bureau also reported that "the estimate of U.S. retail e-commerce sales for the second quarter of 2007, adjusted for seasonal variation and holiday and trading-day differences, but not for price changes, was $33.6 billion, an increase of 6.4 percent from the first quarter of 2007."

audience and then efficiently and cost-effectively reach it with appropriate marketing, advertising, and public relations efforts.

By 2010, more than 1.8 billion people worldwide are expected to be web surfers, according to the *Computer Industry Almanac*. One of the biggest misconceptions first-time online sellers have is that if they simply create and publish a basic e-commerce website and then start offering products for sale, thousands or millions of web surfers will come flocking to their site with credit cards in hand, ready to place orders.

Well, this is not the case! To launch a successful online business that incorporates an e-commerce website, the site you create must look professional, be easy to navigate, and offer products your customers want and/or need at competitive prices. This is only the start, however. You'll also need to attract web surfers, aka *traffic*, to your e-commerce website and provide top-notch customer service. Then, you'll need to quickly ship the products you sell to your customers and manage the day-to-day operations of your new business.

The Lingo You'll Need to Know

Throughout this book, I'll explain the important terms you'll need to understand to brainstorm, design, create, and manage your website and online business. Here's a quick summary of some key terms that have been used thus far:

➡ *E-commerce turnkey solution*. A complete set of website design and management tools that allows anyone to create, publish, and manage an e-commerce website for a pre-determined (often recurring) fee. These solutions require absolutely no programming knowledge. A computer with access to the internet is required to use them, because the majority of these tools are online-based. See Chapters 5 and 6 for more information about these powerful tools.

➡ *Merchant*. Someone who sells products or services. In terms of this book, it refers to someone selling products online using an e-commerce website.

➡ *E-commerce website*. A website designed to sell products online. This type of website must quickly and accurately convey details about the product(s) being sold, plus have a shopping cart feature that allows customers (web surfers) to safely and securely place their orders using a major credit card or another online payment method. (See Chapter 15 for details about online payment options.)

➡ *Shopping cart.* The module of an e-commerce website that serves as an interactive order form. It allows customers to input their order, shipping details, and credit card/payment information in a secure manner, and then place their order electronically through a website.

➡ *Traffic.* Refers to the number of web surfers who visit your site. A visitor is someone who surfs over to your website to explore. Your goal as an online merchant is to transform web surfers into paying customers who place orders for your product electronically. The percentage of people who go from surfers to paying customers is referred to as your conversion rate.

Running a Successful Online Business

Just about anyone with a basic understanding of computers, a bit of creativity, and knowledge of how to surf the web can start what could become a successful online business. The trick is coming up with a profitable product (or products) to sell, developing a quality, professional-looking website, and then efficiently marketing the website to generate traffic.

Depending on what you're selling, your target audience, and how much marketing you do, your online business can be a part-time project that generates a bit of extra income, or it could potentially be grown into a mega-successful, full-time business venture that allows you to generate a very respectable income over time.

Although this book will help you get started quickly, it does not guarantee or even suggest that you'll make a profit overnight, or even within a few weeks. As you'll discover, once your website is operational it'll take time and effort to properly market it, generate traffic, and attract paying customers. Your ability to earn a profit will be based in large part on what product you're selling, whether there is a demand for your product, and how much competition you have.

Because an online business that utilizes an e-commerce website is relatively easy and inexpensive to create and launch, the barriers to entry are very low. Thus, it's a viable business opportunity for just about anyone looking to earn extra income, including students, homemakers, senior citizens, entrepreneurs, people with disabilities, and anyone who is employed part time or full time. Traditional retailers can also benefit by expanding into cyberspace in order to reach a broader, potentially worldwide, customer base.

Obviously, the more you know about computers, the product you're planning to sell, basic business operations, and marketing, advertising, and public relations, the better off you'll be. But with the help of books like this one, many people have learned these basic principles as they move forward with their online business venture.

Almost Anything Can Be Sold Online

The internet is a powerful tool with thousands of new web surfers coming online each and every day. Each of these web surfers, no matter where in the world they're located, is a potential customer for your business.

If you're already a savvy web surfer, you know that there are well over 100 million websites and over 50 million blogs currently online, with millions more being added every month. Each of these websites is unique and has one or more purposes. For example, a website can be used to

- convey information using text, graphics, photographs, audio, video, animations, and other interactive or multimedia elements.
- provide an interactive entertainment experience, such as an online game.
- provide a forum for exchanging information or ideas with other web surfers (either in real time through an online chat room or by using message boards, blogs, podcasts or videocasts).
- sell information in the form of downloadable content, such as e-books, audio, or video.
- sell a service.
- sell a product.

This book focuses on how to sell tangible products, either retail or wholesale, online. For the purposes of this book, a product is any physical item that can be described, promoted, and sold online, and then shipped to a customer once payment is received. Online merchants have become very creative in terms of the products that can be sold using the internet. In fact, virtually any product you can imagine has already been sold successfully online. The possibilities are truly limitless.

The obvious question, however, is that with so many websites currently online, what opportunities still exist for someone like you to launch a profitable e-commerce website? Well, it's true that large, well-known mass-market retailers, such as Wal-Mart or Target and thousands of well-established, online-only businesses, such as Amazon.com, currently dominate the internet and offer a vast selection of products at low prices to web surfers. These companies also have established customer bases and operating and marketing budgets in the millions of dollars.

For a single individual to be successful selling his or her products online, it may be possible to compete with the big guys by offering lower prices and better customer service, but this approach will dramatically limit your ability to earn a profit from each sale. Thus, the most successful startup online businesses operated by everyday people (as opposed to large businesses) focus on offering products that

→ cater to a niche audience or target customer,
→ can't be readily purchased from mass-market retailers or from a local mall, and
→ are unique, personalized, collectible, or customized for the customer.

Small online business operators have experienced success selling a wide range of products. Just a sampling of items that could be sold using an e-commerce website includes:

→ Antiques
→ Any products that are bundled together, modified, or customized to provide added value to the customer
→ Art
→ Clothing and shoes, especially in hard-to-find sizes
→ Collectibles
→ Crafts and handmade items
→ Gift items, especially items that are customized, engraved, or personalized
→ Hard-to-find tools, items, supplies, and equipment for various hobbies, such as specialty photography equipment, fishing gear, sewing gear, scrapbook-making supplies, and knitting supplies
→ Jewelry (new, antique, hand-crafted, one-of-a-kind, etc.)
→ Specialty items for specific jobs or occupations
→ Used books
→ Used video and computer games
→ Vintage or custom-made clothing

Chapters 2, 9, and 10 focus specifically on how to properly identify and reach the ideal target customer for the product you'll be selling from your e-commerce website. Understanding your audience and being able to effectively address its wants and needs while staying within its budget from a pricing standpoint is essential. The next step, however, involves coming up with a product to sell. That's the focus of Chapter 1.

Getting Started Is Relatively Easy

The title of this book suggests that in less than a week, you can be well on your way to operating a successful e-commerce website. This book assumes that you're starting off with the following resources already in place:

- A fantastic business idea
- One or more products to sell online, with inventory on hand or that's easy to access quickly
- An understanding of your target audience
- A name for your company
- The fundamental structure of the business
- Detailed written descriptions and professional-quality photographs (or video) of the product you'll be selling
- A computer with access to the internet
- A written business, financial, and marketing plan

The various chapters of this book will help you pull these resources together. Once they're in place, you'll learn how to find a turnkey e-commerce solution that within a week or so will allow you to create and publish a basic but professional-looking website capable of selling your products online. Of course, over time, you'll want to fine-tune, expand, and improve your website. After all, your site should be an ever-changing, constantly evolving place in cyberspace that your potential and existing customers want to visit again and again.

Turnkey E-Commerce Solutions

Until recently, if you wanted to launch your own e-commerce website to sell products online, you needed to be a computer guru with a thorough understanding of HTML programming, Java, Flash, and a wide range of other complex programming languages and software-based website design tools. You also needed to invest weeks, often months, to create from scratch a website capable of handling the functionality needed to securely sell products online. Of course, a team of programmers and graphic designers could also be hired (at a significant expense) to do much of the programming for you, but as the website operator, you still needed a good understanding of website design and programming.

These days, however, a handful of well-known companies offer complete e-commerce turnkey solutions that allow ordinary people with no programming or graphic design knowledge whatsoever to utilize a set of easy-to-use tools and professionally designed templates to effortlessly design and publish awesome looking and extremely powerful websites in a matter of hours, not days or months. Best of all, many of these turnkey solutions have a very low startup cost—often under $100.

These solutions also include the tools needed to begin accepting orders and online credit card payments for those orders. In other words, you don't necessarily need to set up a costly credit card merchant account with a local bank or financial institution to begin accepting Visa, MasterCard, American Express, or Discover credit card or debit card payments. This alone eliminates a significant barrier to entry.

Design and Launch an E-Commerce Website in One Week focuses on just a few of the complete e-commerce turnkey solutions currently available. Depending on your level of experience, website design knowledge, your product, and your personal preferences, and the information provided in Chapters 5 and 6, you should be able to select and start using a turnkey e-commerce solution that meets your wants and needs. Some of the products you'll learn about are available from companies, such as Yahoo!, eBay.com, Google, and GoDaddy.com.

Even with the most advanced and powerful e-commerce turnkey solutions that utilize the best, most eye-catching website design templates, you'll still need to create professional quality text and incorporate professional-looking photos and other graphic elements (referred to as *assets*) into your website to ensure it can help you achieve your goals. Basically, to compete effectively, your website needs to look and function as well, if not better, than those your competition offers. Of course, you must also offer products that your customers want or need to purchase.

To achieve these objectives, you may want to hire the services of a professional freelance writer to write your product descriptions and promotional

CLICK TIP

Need to hire an experienced and professional writer, programmer, website designer, photographer, or graphic artist? The eLance.com (elance.com) website allows you to post your needs and have freelance professionals bid on the work.

copy, and a professional photographer to take top-quality product shots for your website. As you proceed, you might also want to hire a professional graphic designer to create a logo for your company and an overall look for your website that's visually unique and appealing to your visitors. Finding and hiring professional help is covered in Chapter 4.

E-Commerce vs. Traditional Retail

Although a traditional retail store can sell the same products as a website, there are major differences between operating a traditional *bricks-and-mortar retail store* and an e-commerce website. Most importantly, traditional stores are more expensive to run. Just some of the costs and drawbacks associated with operating a traditional bricks-and-mortar retail store include:

➡ having to purchase, lease, or rent the retail space that is a storefront, at a cost of hundreds or thousands of dollars per month.

➡ the need to hire employees and managers to staff the store.

➡ having to purchase and maintain plenty of inventory.

➡ having to purchase store fixtures, displays, point-of-sale merchandising materials, signage, cash registers, etc.

➡ defined operating hours.

➡ customers confined to a specific geographic area or region, because it has a fixed location.

➡ overall startup costs in the tens of thousands or hundreds of thousands of dollars, and sometimes more.

➡ a single, stand-alone, mom-and-pop store faces competition with mass-market retailers and chain stores in local markets.

➡ the tremendous risk involved in opening a traditional retail store as a startup business.

On the other hand, operating an e-commerce business offers a wide range of benefits. They include:

→ very low startup and overhead costs.

→ a potential worldwide customer base.

→ the ability to accept orders and promote products 24 hours per day, 365 days per year, because a website is always open and available to web surfers.

→ a flexible work schedule.

→ smaller inventory requirements.

→ the ability to operate from almost anywhere, such as from a home or small office/warehouse location.

→ the ability to create a website that's as professional looking as those operated by large, well-established, multimillion dollar companies, thus leveling the playing field.

→ an e-commerce website that can be created and open for business in hours or days, not months or years.

→ very low financial risk (in the hundreds or thousands of dollars).

→ the ability to sell virtually any product—from yachts to pet supplies— that can be sold in a traditional retail environment.

Plan on Making an Ongoing Investment in Time and Money

You already know that starting and operating a successful e-commerce website is not a get-rich-quick scheme. For your online business to become truly profitable, you'll need to invest a significant amount of time, resources, and money on an ongoing basis to build, establish, maintain, and grow your business. The success of your business then depends on a constant flow of traffic to your website that's comprised of people in your target customer base.

To generate this ongoing traffic, plan on spending money on advertising, marketing, and public relations efforts, and on investing the time necessary to properly and cost effectively implement these efforts while also handling the other day-to-day tasks associated with the operation of your business. Some of these responsibilities are:

→ Acquiring and maintaining inventory

→ Processing and shipping orders

➡ Handling returns
➡ Updating and improving your website constantly
➡ Managing your company's financial records (bookkeeping)
➡ Planning, designing, implementing, and managing the promotional campaigns designed to promote your website and product
➡ Handling customer-service issues

Like any business, starting an online business involves some level of risk. Thus, you'll typically want to start off on a smaller scale and gradually build up your business. Think twice before quitting your current job and giving up your stable income to launch an online business.

An online business can usually start off as a small, part-time project where you work evenings or on weekends and slowly grow. Only when it becomes stable and profitable should you consider making this your full-time career.

Also, always have an exit strategy in place as you move forward. If your online business fails, how will you and your family handle the financial ramifications? You'll soon discover that there are strategies you can implement to avoid unnecessary financial hardship or bankruptcy should your business fail or take longer than expected to become successful.

Whether you're starting a traditional business or an online one, when you get right down to it, a business is a business. Thus, as you establish your online business, you'll want to follow the same basic steps you would for any business. This means starting off by creating a detailed and well-thought-out business plan that includes details about your business, its goals, financial projections, market research, and other details that provide a road map for

CLICK TIP

For help creating a detailed business plan, check out the Business Plan Pro software from PaloAlto Software (paloalto.com). The $99.95 Standard Edition (for Windows) of this software offers an interactive, step-by-step business plan guide, plus more than 500 sample plans and a variety of other useful resources. The U.S. Small Business Administration offers free tools and advice for writing business plans. Point your web browser to sba.gov/smallbusinessplanner/plan/writeabusiness plan/index.html.

you to follow as you move forward. This is an important step that should not be skipped!

What's Covered Here

Chapter 1 will help you begin choosing what product or products to sell online, and then in Chapter 2, you'll discover the importance of understanding and being able to effectively reach your target audience. In Chapter 3, the initial steps involved in starting an online business are explained. In Chapter 4, you'll begin learning about the tools and services available to help you get started quickly and inexpensively. You'll also learn how to register your website's URL (its address in cyberspace).

Chapter 5 provides an overview of the e-commerce turnkey solutions available to online business operators that can help you quickly create a professional-looking website with no programming knowledge or experience.

In Chapter 6, you'll find details about specific popular and well-established e-commerce turnkey solutions. The companies and services described, however, are just a sampling of what's available.

Because every online-based business should contain specific information and content, Chapter 7 helps you better understand website design fundamentals and helps you gather and create the core content for your site. Chapter 8 describes some of the online payment processing options available to you as a merchant.

Once you understand that designing and publishing a professional-looking website is just part of the formula for success, Chapters 9 and 10 will help you properly promote your website and business using a comprehensive, multifaceted approach that involves public relations, marketing, promotions, and advertising.

In Chapter 11, important concepts about how to manage the day-to-day operations of your business are explored. The in-depth interviews with e-commerce experts in Chapter 12 will be extremely valuable as you move forward with your online business venture.

Each chapter contains special features to increase your understanding of the topics covered. Sidebars highlight tips and concepts that are especially important to building a successful business. And each chapter lists important, often online, resources you can use to learn more about a specific topic.

Let's Get Started!

If you already think you have what it takes to become a successful online business operator; you're ready to invest the time, energy, and finances necessary to get started; you have some good ideas about what you might like to sell; and you know the target audience you're interested in reaching, then you're well on your way to achieving success!

The internet offers limitless potential to market and sell products to an ever-expanding and worldwide audience of consumers. Never before has launching and operating an online business been such a viable opportunity for so many people just like you!

Chapter 1

Choosing a Product to Sell

*B*efore you go through the effort of creating a website, it's essential to decide what product or products you'll ultimate be selling online. (For simplicity's sake, "product" is considered to include "products.") That's the focus of this chapter. While virtually any tangible product can be sold online, there are a handful of things you'll want to consider as you determine what product(s) you should sell through your website in order to generate profits.

Initially the product you have in mind to sell may seem extremely viable, but after considering all of the necessary factors, you may discover that an opportunity you thought existed might not be as lucrative as you would have hoped. This, unfortunately, is extremely common. Thus, it could take you weeks, maybe months, to find the perfect product to sell online.

Consider Your Existing Competition in Cyberspace

Don't kid yourself. You're not the first entrepreneur to think of starting an online business selling a particular product. In fact, if you do some research, chances are you'll find competition offering identical or similar products to what you're thinking about selling. Assuming this is the case, how will you set your website and its product apart? What added value will you offer? Think realistically about why people should shop at your website, as opposed to buying from your competition.

One of the biggest mistakes you can make is focusing exclusively on offering the lowest price possible for your product. While you'll be able to undercut your competition in the short term, there will always be a competitor who can offer even lower prices. This dramatically cuts your profit margin. With lower profits, you'll earn less money for yourself, and you probably won't earn the funds needed to properly market and grow your business in the future.

Although you always want your prices to be competitive, you don't necessarily want or need to offer the absolute lowest prices on the internet. Depending on the product, people are often willing to pay extra if you offer superior customer service, have an easy-to-use website that makes ordering easy, or if you somehow add value to what you're selling. People will also pay a premium for hard-to-find products or highly collectible items.

As you develop the plans for your business, pay careful attention to what your existing competition is doing. Focus on what you can do better and how you can better serve the wants and needs of your target customer base. Also, consider what competition is likely to appear in the near future.

For example, if you're planning to sell a new product that you believe will be the next ultratrendy, gotta-have-it item, like Beanie Babies,® charm bracelets, or Crocs® shoes, you can bet that within a few weeks, your competition both online and in the real world will be fierce. Will you be able to complete with companies willing and able to spend more money than you on

CLICK TIP

Once you pinpoint a product you might be interested in selling, tap your skills as a web surfer and seek out websites and companies that are currently selling the same or similar products. Discover who your online competition is or will be. Use search engines like Google and Yahoo!, and enter a wide range of different search phrases (using product names, product categories, product descriptions, and company names). Be sure to check shopping and price comparison websites like nextag.com as well as online mass-market retailers, such as Amazon.com. As you discover who your competitors are, spend time surfing their websites to determine how you might do things better or differently.

marketing and advertising, or who are able to purchase their inventory in much larger quantities in order to keep their costs down?

Seek Out Your Existing Real-World Competition

If your product can be sold in cyberspace, chances are it's also profitable for traditional retail stores and mail order catalogs to offer. If the product you're offering is available at local stores, why should people shop online, wait at least several days to receive their order, and pay extra for shipping? In addition, if the item is readily available through traditional retail outlets, you'll need to compete from a pricing standpoint.

For startup online businesses, the best products to offer are ones that are unique, customizable, collectible, handcrafted, or *not* readily available through local retail stores, mall stores, or mass-market retailers, such as Wal-Mart or Target. Ideally, the product you choose to sell should also be hard to find online.

Determine Your Inventory Requirements

Based on your sales projections, determine much inventory you need to maintain in-house in order to process and ship your orders immediately upon receiving them. If you'll be selling high-ticket items, can you initially afford to maintain the level of inventory you'll need?

Once you determine how much inventory you need on hand at any given time, you want to focus on the accessibility of that inventory. How long will it take you to establish and then replenish your inventory as needed?

If an item needs to be imported from overseas or manufactured from scratch, reorders could take weeks or months. If you're purchasing inventory directly from a wholesaler, manufacturer, or distributor, what happens if your product becomes backordered and unavailable? Will you be able to acquire the product elsewhere at a competitive price?

Can you purchase your inventory in sufficient quantities to qualify for discounts to keep your costs low? Is there a sufficient quantity of the item available to you to meet the demands of your customers? One of the worst and most costly mistakes you can make is to market a product, generate a significant demand for it, and then not be able to fulfill your orders because you can't get your hands on ample inventory. So when calculating your inventory needs, be sure to consider how long it takes to replenish that inventory, and then order accordingly. You don't want to sell out prematurely and have to turn customers away.

Calculate Your Costs

The ideal formula for a successful retail or e-commerce business is to be able to purchase or acquire your inventory for the absolute lowest cost-per-unit possible and then resell those products at the highest retail price possible in order to generate a profit. No matter what quantity you're buying, always know what your cost-per-unit is, and make sure there's enough profit margin to cover all of your operating expenses (including, for example, your own salary, the cost of operating your website, and your company's marketing/advertising). Be sure to calculate appropriate shipping charges, sales taxes (if applicable), order processing fees, warehousing costs, packaging costs, insurance, finance charges (interest, etc.), and any other expenses that diminish your profit margins.

You'll quickly discover that in most cases when acquiring inventory, you'll receive the best prices when you seek out quantity discounts. Depending on the product, this might mean ordering dozens, hundreds, or even thousands of the same product at once in order to benefit from the savings offered by a manufacturer, wholesaler, or distributor. When placing larger orders, shipping and warehousing costs go up, so be prepared to do some number crunching to determine what's best for your business.

Some businesspeople rely on credit to acquire their initial inventory. Whether you utilize credit terms from your supplier or use a credit card to purchase inventory, chances are you'll need to pay finance charges and interest, so calculate these additional fees into your per unit pricing.

Depending on what you'll be selling and who you're acquiring your inventory from, don't be afraid to negotiate for the best pricing possible, especially if you're purchasing a significant quantity of an item.

Set Your Pricing

Pricing refers to how much you'll be able to sell your products for to your customers. Your pricing must cover all of your expenses, allow you to generate a profit, but at the same time, be competitive with your competition.

As you'll discover, finding the perfect price point at which to sell your items is a process, and it may require some experimentation. In some cases, you may discover you're able to charge a premium for your product, because of strong demand and limited supply in the marketplace. In other situations, you may find it necessary to discount your items or offer incentives, such as free shipping, in order to compete with your competition and attract customers.

Throughout this process, it's essential that you have a firm grasp on all of your costs and your cost-per-unit so that you can ensure that your company operates in the black. After all, a wide range of factors and unexpected or hidden costs can impact your profit margins.

Another less tangible cost that startup online business owners don't always take into account is the value of their time and what time investment is needed to establish and launch their business, handle the day-to-day operations, and ultimately fill each and every order. When all is said and done, your business should be able to generate enough profit so your take-home pay compensates you for this time investment. Ultimately, your pricing must reflect all of your costs and expenses.

Again, once you calculate all of your costs (based on projections) in advance, set your retail pricing, and do some number crunching based on forecasted sales, you may discover that the product you hoped to sell does not provide a viable opportunity after all.

The Demographics of Your Target Audience

One topic that was mentioned in the Preface, is the focus of Chapter 2, and will be repeated many times in this book is the absolute need to understand and know your target customer, as well as your product. It is one of the keys to success that should not be ignored!

As an online business operator, you must have a thorough understanding of who your target customers are, what they want, what they need, and how what you're offering addresses those wants and needs, or helps to solve a specific problem. The majority of successful startup online businesses tend to cater to a very niche target audience with a specific product that is in demand by that group of people.

Your target audience can be defined in many ways. Just some of the characteristics you can use to carefully define your target audience are:

- Age
- Club or association memberships
- Education level
- Geographic region
- Height
- Hobbies
- Income
- Investing habits
- Marital status
- Medical necessities
- Occupation
- Religion
- Sex
- Sexual orientation
- Special interests
- Spending habits
- Weight

It's common for a target audience to be defined by combining several of these factors. For example, you might determine that the product you'll be selling caters mainly to well-educated, single women, between the ages of 18 and 49, who earn at least $50,000 per year and live in a major city. Then again, you might determine that your target audience is comprised mainly of men,

WARNING

Not everyone is internet savvy and comfortable surfing the web or buying products online using credit cards. Unless your target audience falls into the large and ever-growing group of people with access to the internet, especially those who are comfortable shopping online, you'll find it difficult to generate sales from your website. For example, a senior citizen is less apt to be internet savvy and have access to the internet than a college student or young business professional. On the other hand, current students tend to be very internet savvy but often lack the major credit card or debit card needed to make purchases online.

between the ages of 49 and 60, who are affluent, married, and enjoy playing golf.

Once you know exactly who your primary target audience is, you'll have a much easier time creating a website to sell your products and cater to their wants and needs. You'll also find it easier to create an advertising, marketing, public relations, and promotional campaign that works.

Trying to sell a product to someone who doesn't want or need it is an absolute waste of your time, money, and effort. Again, you'll find it more difficult to sell products that cater to a mass-market audience (i.e., almost everybody) because you'll probably be competing head-on with mass-market retailers, such as Wal-Mart, plus major department stores, chain stores, and other local retailers.

A key to success is to really get to know your target customer base, be able to get inside their heads, and understand their true wants and needs. Next, your objective should be to address those wants and needs with your products in a way that solves a problem or addresses an issue that they're facing.

Figure Out How You'll Reach Your Audience

Once you determine what you'll be selling and who your products will appeal to, you can consider how you'll target that audience with your advertising, marketing, public relations, and promotions—as well as with the actual content of your website. You'll also be able to determine if you'll be able to cost effectively reach this audience and drive them to your website, or if getting its attention will simply cost too much or require resources that are not at your disposal.

The big question on your mind should be how will you drive potential customers who fall within your target audience to your website. Then, once they're at your website, how will you transform them into paying customers? In reality, the process of capturing web surfers' attention with your website's content must happen in mere seconds, or your visitors will simply surf elsewhere.

If you understand your audience, know what it's looking for, and can quickly and succinctly address its needs, wants, and concerns on your website (while at the same time promoting a sense of professionalism and confidence in your business), you're more apt to generate a sale. Chapter 7 focuses on how to design a website that appeals to your customers.

Forecast the Current and Future Demand for Your Product

For your online business to have long-term success potential, you want to offer products that are in demand today and that will continue to be in demand in the months, and hopefully years, to come. Through market research, you should be able to determine how quickly your target audience is growing (or shrinking) and whether or not your online business will continue to be viable in six months, one year, three years, five years and over the long-term.

HAVING A PASSION FOR YOUR PRODUCTS IS VERY HELPFUL

As a general rule, you're more apt to achieve success if you wind up selling products you truly believe in, that you're highly knowledgeable about, and that you have a passion for. For example, if you're an avid fisherman, selling specialty fishing gear to fellow enthusiasts will be more enjoyable for you than selling products in which you have little or no interest.

Again, determining the future potential demand for your product requires a very good understanding of the product itself as well as your target audience, your competition, and any changes that may happen in the marketplace over time. In the future, people's buying habits may change, as will their wants and needs. As a businessperson, not only do you need to understand this concept, you must also be able to plan for it and transform your business accordingly to keep up with current and future trends.

> ## CLICK TIP
>
> One way to find the perfect product to sell is to first focus on what interests you, and then consider what types of unique or hard-to-find (non-mass-market) items you personally tend to purchase.

If you determine that in one year, the demand for your proposed product will be diminished, that gives you a relatively small window during which to build up your business and generate a profit before you'll need to abandon the business or dramatically change its focus. Establishing a business requires time, money, and resources. You don't want your investment to go to waste by selecting products to sell that don't have the ongoing potential to generate the profits you're striving for.

Finding Potential Products to Sell

Now that you have an idea about the factors you want to consider before committing yourself to selling a specific product online, the next step is to really focus on the product you have in mind to sell and make sure it's viable. The Preface gave a detailed list of items and product categories that tend to sell well on websites created by startup online business operators.

If you're searching for potential products to sell, the following list provides resources for finding wholesalers, distributors, and manufacturers that supply products you could sell online. Of course, you could also manufacture, customize, or create your own unique or one-of-a-kind products, for example, which also tend to sell well online. As you search for potential items to sell, take advantage of these resources:

➡ *Crafters.* Selling handcrafted, one-of-a-kind, and/or unique items of any type, for example, jewelry, gift items, artwork, and clothing usually offers a good opportunity for online sales. Check out local craft shows and festivals to find unique items that you believe would appeal to people shopping online.

➡ *Drop-shipper directories.* A drop shipper is a distributor that offers a large selection of products. It sells the products to its dealers at wholesale prices. However, the drop shipper directly ships all items to your customers (on your behalf) so you never have to acquire any inventory. Your job is simply to market the items and take orders. Before deciding to work with a drop shipper, you'll want to make sure it's reputable, reliable, and offers quality products. To find a listing of drop shippers, use any internet search engine and enter the search term "dropshippers" or "drop shippers."

➡ *Garage sales and flea markets.* These are particularly useful if you want to focus on selling antiques, collectibles, or vintage items. Attending these events also helps you determine what products sell well and who's buying them.

➡ *Importers.* These are companies that import products in large quantities from overseas manufacturers but often don't handle retail distribution themselves. An importer acts as the middleman between manufacturer and retailers, and sometimes offers products that can't be purchased elsewhere. Many importers, however, require you to place large orders for specific products. Dealing with importers requires a bit more knowledge about business, foreign markets, currency conversion, and international (freight) shipping. The profit margins, however, are potentially higher if you deal with an importer, as opposed to a wholesaler or distributor based in America. Kompass (kompass-usa.com) offers an online directory of importers and exporters that is searchable by product name or category, or by company name.

➡ *Local businesses and manufacturers.* You may discover the perfect item to sell online by visiting local shops, boutiques, and stores. If an item is selling well at a local retail store, chances are it will also sell online to a potentially worldwide market. Once you do pinpoint a product to sell, you can track down its manufacturer or find a wholesaler/distributor that supplies it to local retailers.

➡ *Search eBay.com and Overstock.com.* By spending time on eBay.com or Overstock.com, for example, you can learn more about what types of items and products are selling, at what price points, and what level of demand exists for those items. Overstock.com and eBay.com can also be excellent sources for acquiring inventory at highly competitive prices, especially if you're seeking quantities of discontinued or overstock items.

➡ *Trade shows.* Every industry has its own trade shows where product developers, manufacturers, wholesalers, and distributors get together to show off their latest offerings. Attending trade shows can help you find products to sell and meet with suppliers. To find trade shows scheduled for your area (or anywhere in the world for that matter), check out the *Tradeshow Week* (tradeshowweek.com), EventsEye (eventseye.com), or BizTrade (biztradeshows.com) websites. You can also contact local convention centers in your city to see what events each will be hosting in the months ahead or look at the Calendar or Events section of any industry trade publication.

➡ *Wholesale directories.* These are directories of wholesalers and distributors who represent product manufacturers and act as the middle man between manufacturers and retailers. There are a variety of directories available that list wholesalers and distributors by industry or product category, which makes tracking them down relatively easy. Using any search engine, enter the search phrase "wholesaler directory" to find referrals that offer the types of products you want to sell.

What's Next

As an online business owner, one of the biggest challenges you face is coming up with a viable product to sell online. Once you've narrowed down your options, however, putting together a well-designed e-commerce website to effectively market and sell your product is a relatively straightforward process. Your own creativity is needed, however, when searching for the ideal product to sell, when designing your website, and then when marketing your product (and your website) to your target customers. Getting to know your audience is essential, and it's the focus of Chapter 2.

Getting to Know Your Target Audience

*R*egardless of what you'll be selling online, identifying your target market and determining how to reach it are critical. To do so effectively, you should

➥ understand who comprises your target market;

➥ know how to effectively reach your target market with your website as well as with your advertising, marketing, public relations, and promotions; and

➡ properly cater to your target market's wants and needs.

This chapter helps you define your target audience, pinpoint the audience your website will cater to, and decide how you'll best reach that market. Remember, it's to your benefit to know and understand as much about your target customer as possible. Understanding your market typically requires you to conduct research.

Ultimately, as you begin to develop your website's content as well as your marketing materials (and product packaging, if applicable), you'll want to put yourself in your target customers' shoes and think the way they think. If you're a middle-age male targeting young, single females with your products, this might pose more of a challenge than catering to an audience you readily relate to and with whom you share many common interests.

Establish Your Niche

When starting out, most online business owners find it infinitely easier to sell products that cater to a small niche market. It is easier to understand the potential customer base, address its wants, needs, and concerns, and specifically focus your website's content and your marketing materials on this narrowly-defined audience.

A niche market can be any group of people that you define as your target audience. It can be based on a single defining factor, such as a special interest. For example, if you're selling a unique new golf accessory, the single criteria you might use to define your target audience is avid golfers or golf enthusiasts. You can more narrowly define this audience by focusing on just male or female golfers, golfers who earn a specific income, golfers who live or play golf in a specific geographic region, golfers who are members of a private golf club, golfers who are retired, or golfers who are left-handed.

The more narrowly you define your audience, the easier it is to ascertain its wants and needs and then to focus your website's content and your product marketing to those people. Of course, your product might appeal to several unique target audiences, in which case, you'd want to define and address each of these audiences separately in order to maximize your customer base and the sales potential for your product. It's always a good strategy, however, to begin by focusing on what you believe to be the biggest and easier target audience to reach and then broaden your efforts as your online business becomes more established.

Very few products appeal to everyone. The few products that do are considered mass-market products and are most likely already being sold at traditional retail stores, mass-market retailers, and department stores, and by many online merchants. Again, the products you should be looking to sell need to be unique, hard to find, customized, and/or not readily available at retail.

CLICK TIP

As you do your product research, keep a written list of the most common questions people have about the product. You'll want to address these questions on your website and in your marketing materials. In Chapter 7, for example, you'll learn why creating and posting a product FAQ (Frequently Asked Questions) document on your site is beneficial. (It can save you a lot of time answering e-mails and phone calls from individual customers.)

Before you can define your niche market, however, spend as much time as is necessary to get to know absolutely everything about the product you'll be selling. Learn all about its uses, features, and benefits. Discover what it is about the product that appeals to people, and understand what its drawbacks are so you can properly address them. Also, invest the time needed to learn about competing products so you can explain exactly why your product is superior, more useful, more cost-effective, more efficient, and/or packed with more features. In a nutshell, you want to become an expert on your product. By the time you start selling it, you should be able to answer absolutely any question about it.

Defining Your Audience

You already know how important it is to understand and know your target audience. Use Figure 2.1: Target Audience Worksheet to help you fine-tune exactly who comprises this customer base. Think about what your product is, to whom it primarily appeals, who purchases it, who uses it, what needs it addresses, how it potentially solves a problem, and who benefits the most from using it.

Figure 2.1: **TARGET AUDIENCE WORKSHEET**

Directions: For each category, check all that apply specifically to your primary target audience. Once you've carefully narrowed down your target audience, complete this worksheet a second time to define the secondary audience for your product.

Gender: ❑ Male ❑ Female ❑ Not applicable

Marital Status: ❑ Single ❑ Married ❑ Divorced
❑ Widowed ❑ Not applicable

Age: ❑ Child ❑ Teenager ❑ Age 18 to 24
❑ Age 25 to 49 ❑ Age 50 to 65 ❑ Age 66+
❑ Not applicable

Race: ❑ White ❑ African American ❑ Hispanic
❑ Asian ❑ Other:_____ ❑ Not applicable

**Sexual
Orientation:** ❑ Straight ❑ Gay ❑ Bisexual ❑ Not applicable

Income Level: ❑ Under $15,000 per year
❑ $15,001 to $25,000 per year
❑ $25,001 to $45,000 per year
❑ $45,001 to $55,000 per year
❑ $55,001 to $99,999 per year
❑ $100,000 to $500,000 per year
❑ $500,000 to $999,999 per year
❑ $1,000,000+ per year
❑ Not applicable

Education Level: ❑ Some high school
❑ High school graduate
❑ College graduate
❑ Advanced degree
❑ Not applicable

Figure 2.1: **TARGET AUDIENCE WORKSHEET,** continued

Occupation: _____ ❑ Not applicable

Religion: _____ ❑ Not applicable

Geographic

Region: Specific City/State—Specify: _____
- ❑ United States
- ❑ Canada
- ❑ Europe
- ❑ Asia
- ❑ South America
- ❑ North America
- ❑ Africa
- ❑ Australia
- ❑ Antartica
- ❑ Not applicable

Physical

Attributes:
- ❑ Tall
- ❑ Short
- ❑ Average height
- ❑ Thin
- ❑ Overweight
- ❑ Average weight
- ❑ Not applicable

Housing:
- ❑ Owns home
- ❑ Rents home
- ❑ Rents apartment
- ❑ Owns condo
- ❑ Rents condo
- ❑ Lives with parents
- ❑ Lives with roommate(s)

Figure 2.1: **TARGET AUDIENCE WORKSHEET,** continued

Housing:
- ❑ Lives with spouse
- ❑ Lives with spouse and children
- ❑ Other: _____
- ❑ Not applicable

Primary Computer and Internet Usage:
- ❑ At home
- ❑ At work
- ❑ Internet café/Wi-fi location
- ❑ Wireless PDA or Smartphone
- ❑ Not online

Hobbies/ Special Interests: _____ ❑ Not applicable

Club/Association Membership: _____ ❑ Not applicable

Spending/ Shopping Habits:
- ❑ Typically shops at retail stores
- ❑ Shops often via mail order
- ❑ Comfortable shopping online
- ❑ Readily uses credit cards
- ❑ Readily uses a debit card
- ❑ Writes checks for purchases
- ❑ Possess a PayPal account
- ❑ Has below average or no credit

Driving Habits:
- ❑ Drives a compact vehicle/hatchback
- ❑ Drives an SUV or van
- ❑ Drives a pick-up truck
- ❑ Drives a sports car

Figure 2.1: **TARGET AUDIENCE WORKSHEET,** continued

Driving Habits:
- ❏ Drives a luxury sedan
- ❏ Drives a hybrid vehicle
- ❏ Owns their vehicle
- ❏ Leases their vehicle
- ❏ Drives less than 15,000 miles per year
- ❏ Drives more than 15,000 miles per year
- ❏ Commutes daily to work
- ❏ Carpools
- ❏ Other: _____

Media Habits:
- ❏ Primarily watches TV
- ❏ Primarily reads newspapers
- ❏ Primarily reads magazines
- ❏ Primarily surfs the web
- ❏ Not applicable

Other Relevant Attribute: _____

Other Relevant Attribute: _____

Other Relevant Attribute: _____

Product-Related Questions

After defining your primary and secondary audience for your product using the Target Audience Worksheet, answer the questions in Figure 2.2: Product Appeal Worksheet as they apply to what you'll be selling and to whom you'll be selling. As you answer these questions on a separate sheet of paper, be as specific as possible. And don't forget to put yourself in your target customer's shoes and think the way they would think (taking into account their needs, wants, and concerns).

Figure 2.2: **PRODUCT APPEAL WORKSHEET**

- What about your product will appeal to your target audience? (Be sure to list specific features, functions, selling points, etc.)

- How will your target customer use the product?

- When will your target customer use the product?

- Why will your target customer use the product?

- What needs does your product address?

- How does your product satisfy your target customer's wants?

- Why would someone want to buy your product?

- What problems, challenges, or obstacles can your product help the customer overcome? How will it make their lives happier, better, easier, less stressful, more entertaining, etc.?

- What are the biggest and best benefits or features that your product offers?

- Describe why your product is worth the money people will spend for it.

- Why should someone use your product as opposed to a competing product?

- What do you anticipate are the biggest objections your target audience will have regarding your product? How can these objections be overcome?

- What misconceptions might your target audience have about your product? What information will you need to convey to help them overcome these misconceptions quickly?

- Why should someone purchase the product from your online business?

Based on the information you compiled in this worksheet, you should now have a relatively detailed profile of your primary customer base as well as your secondary markets. Now, you can proceed by learning as much as possible about the people who make up your target market and begin formulating all of the ways your product addresses its wants and needs.

Doing Your Market Research

Approach your market research from several angles. First, focus on the product you'll be selling and learn as much as you can about the people it appeals to. Research what your competition is doing to market the same or similar products. What approach are your competitors taking? Who are their target audiences? What primary marketing messages are they using to sell the product? Based on your knowledge of the product and your target audience, how can you improve or build on what your competition is doing in order to attract your own customers?

Next, do as much research about your target audience as possible. Based on the profile you create for the people you believe are your primary audience, learn as much as possible about their likes and dislikes, their wants, their needs, and the problems they're facing in their daily lives. Focus on how you can use this knowledge to generate as much interest in your product as possible. How much effort do you have to put into educating your target customer about your product? What information do you need to convey? What is the best way to convey this information in a succinct, easy-to-understand, and cost-effective way that will capture your target audience's attention?

The internet itself is an extremely powerful market research tool. Also, take a close look at whatever information is available from the manufacturers or distributors of the product you're planning to sell (if applicable), as well as whatever materials and information are available from your competition.

Addressing the Wants and Needs of Your Customers

No matter what you're selling, every consumer buys products based on needs or desires. When you are about to begin selling one or more products online, it's important to understand that the need your customer has for a product can be real or it can be perceived. In other words, the consumer might really and truly need the product, or with the help of your marketing, he can become convinced that he needs it in order to solve a problem, make his life somehow easier, or add happiness to his life on some level. This is a perceived need, and it can be just as powerful as a real need in terms of influencing buying habits. Your goal is to make the consumer think, "I need this now!" and get them to ask themselves, "How did I ever live without it?"

In addition to needs, people have wants and desires. Most people have some discretionary income they can use to make purchases that can satisfy

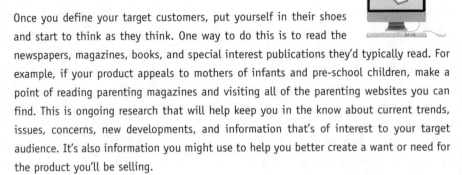

CLICK TIP

Once you define your target customers, put yourself in their shoes and start to think as they think. One way to do this is to read the newspapers, magazines, books, and special interest publications they'd typically read. For example, if your product appeals to mothers of infants and pre-school children, make a point of reading parenting magazines and visiting all of the parenting websites you can find. This is ongoing research that will help keep you in the know about current trends, issues, concerns, new developments, and information that's of interest to your target audience. It's also information you might use to help you better create a want or need for the product you'll be selling.

these various wants and desires. All marketing and advertising is designed to appeal either to a consumer's wants or needs (or both). If a want or need doesn't actually exist for a product you're selling, it becomes your job to create a perceived want or need in the customer's mind, which can be tricky. Executives at advertising agencies, marketing firms, and public relations firms spend years fine-tuning their skills and mastering techniques for influencing peoples' buying habits. Assuming you don't have the budget to hire an advertising agency or public relations firm to help you market and sell your products, these are skills you'll have to learn yourself. The information in Chapter 9 will help get you started.

The approach you take, however, must be customized for the product you're selling and for the audience you're intending to sell your products to. A certain website design, for example, may work extremely well for selling one specific product to a specific target audience, but it might not work at all for another product designed to reach a different audience altogether.

One of the most powerful aspects of selling products on the internet using an e-commerce website is that in addition to using well-written text (referred to as *copy*) to advertise, describe, and promote your product and educate consumers about it, you can also use eye-catching photographs, colorful graphic images, sounds, music, video, graphic animations, as well as other interactive multimedia elements and content.

The internet is interactive, which makes it a potentially far more powerful selling tool than a traditional and passive (noninteractive) newspaper or

CLICK TIP

Another way to get to know your target audience is to spend time with them in person. If you'll be selling to golfers, spend time interacting with golf enthusiasts at golf courses, at pro shops, at trade shows, at golf resorts, and anywhere else you can find the people you believe fit into your target audience. The more time you spend with people in your target audience, the more obvious their wants and needs will become, and the easier it will be for you to address them as you market and sell your product.

magazine ad, television commercial, billboard, or radio commercial. Even though a wide range of online elements can be used expertly to sell your product online, they must be used effectively to truly have an impact on your customer. A bunch of flashy bells and whistles on a website may look amazing but make your site confusing to navigate or say little or nothing about what you're actually selling. That is virtually useless.

Discovering the best ways to utilize the power of the internet and design a professional-looking website that caters to your target audience is covered within Chapter 7. However, before you can design your website and launch your advertising campaign to promote your products and your site, you must

CLICK TIP

Learning how to create a perceived need for a product is a skill and an art form that writers, hosts (pitchmen), and producers of television infomercials and shopping networks have mastered. As you begin to acquire these skills for yourself in order to better market your product online, learn from the masters by watching infomercials on TV. You'll quickly begin wondering how you've ever lived without whatever the pitchman is selling, and you'll probably feel yourself being driven to call the toll-free number and place an order. It's that sense of importance, excitement, urgency, and craving that you ultimately want to create using your website when you begin to promote and sell your product.

first understand exactly who you're trying to reach and then determine the best approach for effectively reaching them.

The approach you take to promote and sell a product online to a college student who has grown up watching MTV and playing video games in New York City, for example, is very different from the approach you'd use to sell a product to a 65-year-old male from Iowa or a single mother from Texas. Each of these people may use the internet and may want what you're selling, but each has vastly different wants and needs.

Reaching Your Customers and Driving Them to Your Website

During your website's design phase, it's essential that every element and piece of content incorporated into your site be created to cater to your target audience. Just because you have the ability to add flashy design to your site (using graphic animations, sound effects, and other elements), it does not mean that you should do so, unless it helps you quickly and effectively communicate your sales message and create a demand for what you're selling. A professional-looking website doesn't have to be overly complex in order to achieve its objectives. In fact, more often than not, from a website design standpoint, simple, straightforward, easy-to-understand, and simple-to-navigate is often better and more effective as a sales tool.

Likewise, as you begin to market your products and drive traffic to your website, you want to use proven and cost-efficient marketing, advertising, public relations, and promotional methods that you believe your target audience will relate to and, more importantly, respond to favorably. As consumers, we're bombarded by advertising messages everywhere, virtually every waking hour of the day. We see and hear advertising messages on TV, on the radio, in print ads, on billboards, in junk mail, in online advertising, and on T-shirts and apparel worn by everyday people. We are also accustomed to tuning these messages out.

Thus, it's become that much more difficult for someone trying to market and sell a product to capture the attention of her target audience, especially in a low-cost, efficient way. Because you probably can't afford to launch a multimillion dollar television campaign to drive traffic to your website, you'll need to find innovative, creative, and affordable ways to capture the attention of your target audience, create a demand for your product, and get those people to place orders on your website.

As an online businessperson, one of your goals should be to become an expert at low-cost, grassroots marketing techniques that allow you to reach a niche audience comprised specifically of people who'd be interested in what you're selling.

What's Next

Now that you've begun thinking about what and to whom you'll be selling, the next step is to focus on what you need to get started in your online business. That's the focus of Chapter 3.

The Tools You'll Need to Get Started Selling Online

*B*y now you realize that a lot goes into finding the perfect product to sell and then pinpointing that perfect target market for that product. Once these important steps are completed, you're ready to start establishing your online business's infrastructure and developing the website you'll use to market and sell your product.

This chapter briefly outlines the tools you'll need to move forward—to establish your business and get it online. By defining your needs early on in the process, you'll more easily be able to create a pre-liminary budget for your startup.

Keep in mind that the steps for establishing the infrastructure for your business outlined in this chapter will take most people more than one day to complete. Plan on spending up to several weeks laying the groundwork for your business and creating its infrastructure. Part of this process involves determining how your business will operate on a day-to-day basis, what tools and services will be used, and what methods you'll utilize to handle important tasks, such as credit card payment and order processing, as well as order fulfillment and bookkeeping. Because every business's needs are totally different, it's important to properly research and understand your options and then choose solutions that best fit your unique needs and budget.

Gathering the Equipment You'll Need

Because you're going to be using the internet to establish a virtual home for your store and tap the millions of web surfers out there to be among your potential customers, you'll need a PC or Mac computer with access to the internet.

Depending on your lifestyle and budget, you may opt to purchase a desktop computer and set up a formal home office. There are countless great deals to be had on state-of-the-art desktop computers from local computer retailers and office supply superstores, as well as online.

For a new, PC desktop computer, plan on spending under $1,000, or a bit more if you also need peripherals and software. Mac desktop computers from Apple (apple.com) tend to cost a bit more. Laptop computers (which are truly portable) typically cost more than otherwise comparable desktop computers. A new PC laptop computer that runs Windows Vista, will cost $600 to $1,500. A MacBook from Apple is priced starting at $1,100. Using a laptop computer gives you mobility and allows you to manage your business from virtually anywhere (as long as access to the internet is available).

In addition to the computer itself, you'll need software. Microsoft Office, for example, offers word processing, spreadsheet management, and a range of other applications. You might also want to invest in accounting or bookkeeping software, such as QuickBooks (Intuit Software) or Microsoft Money (Microsoft) to help manage your business' finances. The finance software you use should be able to print invoices and packing slips for your customers.

Special software to help you manage a database of your customers, suppliers, and other important business contacts is also extremely useful. Microsoft Outlook (part of Microsoft Office), Act! (Sage Software), FileMaker Pro (FileMaker), or the Address Book software that comes bundled with Mac computers can be used for this purpose.

Based on what you'll be selling, you might need to take and edit your own product photos for your website. For this, you'll need software, such as Adobe PhotoShop CS3 (or CS4) or Photoshop Elements (a scaled-down version of PhotoShop). Depending on the tools you use to develop and maintain your website, you may need to acquire off-the-shelf website design and publishing software. Adobe offers products that are considered industry standard for website design, creation, and publishing. If you don't already have the core suite of applications you'll need, plan on spending between $500 and $2,500 for software.

Another part of your computer investment will be in peripherals, such as a printer, speakers, scanner, and a data back-up device (such as an external hard drive). Prices vary dramatically for these items. To save money and desk space, consider investing in an all-in-one printer, scanner, fax machine, and photocopier.

When it comes to internet access, you have a variety of options. You can acquire extremely inexpensive dial-up access to the web for under $20 per month. This is a slow connection that cannot utilize many of the internet's multimedia capabilities. Because you'll be running an online business, you'll be better served by obtaining high-speed DSL, Broadband, or FIOS internet access through your local cable television provider, phone company, or internet service provider.

For a high-speed internet connection, plan on spending between $29.95 and $49.95 per month for unlimited access. In addition to this fee, you'll still need to pay a monthly fee for a turnkey website design and e-commerce solution to design, create, and manage your website. See Chapters 5 and 6 for more information on these products, which will cost anywhere from $9.95 to $99.95 (or more) per month. An alternative is to pay a website hosting service a monthly or annual fee to host the site you create from scratch.

As you set up your office, other tools and equipment you'll probably find useful include:

➡ Briefcase

➡ Credit card payment processing equipment and software (if you acquire a credit card merchant account)

CLICK TIP

To give your business added credibility, consider obtaining an incoming toll-free phone number for your business so your perspective and existing customers can easily get in touch with you. You might also want to rent a post office box from your local post office, or obtain a P.O. box from a third-party company, like your local UPS Store, which allows you to promote a street address (as opposed to a P.O. box address) for your business that is not your home address.

- ➡ Desk and desk chair
- ➡ Filing cabinets
- ➡ Floor and desk lamp(s)
- ➡ Office supplies
- ➡ Postage machine and postage scale
- ➡ Printer stand
- ➡ Shipping supplies
- ➡ Telephone
- ➡ Telephone service (including long distance, caller ID, call waiting, voice mail, etc.)
- ➡ Wastepaper basket

Your local office supply superstore, such as OfficeMax, Staples, or Office Depot is a great place to shop for office furniture, equipment, and supplies, although you're apt to find lower prices if you shop online. The Nextag.com price comparison website, for example, is a great place to find what you're looking for at the lowest price possible—whether it's specific computer or consumer electronics equipment, business tools, or office supplies (such as ink or toner for your printer).

During the office setup process, consider where and how you'll store your inventory until it's sold.

CLICK TIP

Once your business grows and becomes successful, you might opt to hire an outside company to accept, handle, and process all of your incoming telephone orders as well as your order fulfillment from your internet orders. This will free up your time, but reduce your profits because you'll need to pay for these services.

Chances are, you'll need to find a climate-controlled, dry environment. This typically rules out most attics and basements. You must be able to safely store your inventory until it's ready to ship, yet at the same time, you want your inventory to be easily accessible. Having to run back and forth to an off-site storage facility will be inconvenient, but it may be necessary if you can't safely store your inventory in your home or apartment.

CLICK TIP

If you'll be storing any inventory until it's sold, seriously consider purchasing separate business insurance that covers losses against lost, theft, or damage. The inventory for your business probably won't be covered by your homeowner's or renter's insurance policy.

Setting Up Your Business

One of the steps involved with setting up an online business is making that business a legal entity in the eyes of the government and IRS. After consulting with your financial advisor and/or attorney, you might opt to set up your business as a sole proprietorship, DBA, partnership, or some type of corporation. No matter which you choose, there is paperwork to fill out and fees to pay in order to obtain any required local, state, and federal business licenses.

Completing the paperwork to establish a corporation is something you can do yourself, or you can hire a lawyer to do it on your behalf. Based on what you'll be selling and your personal situation, the type of corporation you establish will vary.

To learn more about forming a corporation, visit mycorporation.com or incorporate.com. These are independent companies that can help you inexpensively complete the necessary paperwork and establish a corporation or LLC (limited liability corporation) quickly. Your lawyer or accountant can also help with this process.

The laws and fees for establishing a corporation vary by state, as do the benefits (legal and financial) of establishing this type of business entity. The type of corporation you establish also impacts your personal and business tax liabilities in the future.

Another important step is choosing a name for your business. Once the name is selected, you'll want to register your online business' domain name (website address), and you might want to have a company logo designed. Depending on the business name and the unique look of your logo, it may be advisable to copyright and/or trademark your company's name and logo. This is something you can do yourself, or you can hire a lawyer to do on your behalf.

After consulting with your financial planner or accountant and establishing your business, you'll probably want to set up a separate business checking account. Visit several banks and financial institutions to find a bank that offers the most services for the lowest fees.

> **CLICK TIP**
>
>
>
> To learn more about copyrights and trademarks, visit the United States Patent and Trademark Office's website at uspto.gov. The United States Copyright Office's website is copyright.gov. The forms you'll need to file your patent, trademark, and copyright, as well as directions and fees for doing this, can be found on these websites.

Depending on the e-commerce turnkey solution you choose, you may also need to obtain a credit card merchant account from a bank or financial institution. This account allows you to accept credit and debit card payments online or over the telephone. Some of the turnkey solutions described later in this book handle credit card processing on your behalf, so obtaining your own merchant account won't be necessary. More information about payment acceptance options can be found in Chapter 8.

Establishing Your Own Shipping Department

You'll be shipping your products to customers once you begin taking orders, so invest the time to develop a relationship and open a shipping account with your local post office (usps.com) as well as with FedEx (fedex.com), UPS (ups.com), and/or DHL (dhl.com).

Based on what you'll be shipping, the speed at which your packages will need to arrive at their destinations, and the quantity of packages you'll be shipping each day or week, shop around for the best rates.

Keep in mind that most of the shipping companies provide shippers with free supplies (envelopes, boxes, labels, etc.). This is also true of the U.S. Post Office if you're shipping using its Priority Mail or Express Mail services.

Part of the success of your business depends on your ability to create and manage a "shipping department" in order to quickly, efficiently, and cost-effectively process and ship orders to your customers. Having ample shipping supplies and forms on hand will save you time.

CLICK TIP

As a general rule, always ship your orders using a method that allows you to track your packages and obtain proof of delivery.

If you'll be shipping packages with the USPS, consider investing in a postage machine or using the Click-N-Ship service to avoid constant trips to your local post office to buy postage. Check the USPS website for details about this online postage service.

If you'll be using the USPS to do the majority of your shipping, Endicia.com (for Mac users, mac.endicia.com) offers postage printing/ shipping software that uses a DYMO LabelWriter printer (or any laser or inkjet printer) to print U.S. postage and mailing labels with ease. There's a low monthly fee associated with this time-saving service. More information about processing and shipping orders can be found in Chapter 11.

Your Business's Infrastructure

Putting together all of the pieces for your business' infrastructure before you start selling products is essential. If you're not sure how to proceed with any of these initial steps, seek guidance from experienced accountants, lawyers, consultants, and other business professionals. Free and effective consulting is available from a number of organizations.

One free source of business advice is SCORE (800-634-0245, score.org), which is comprised of volunteer (mostly retired) business professionals willing to offer advice and guidance to first-time business operators and entrepreneurs. SCORE's website offers free online tools and resources of interest to new business operators.

The U.S. Small Business Administration's website (sba.gov/smallbusiness planner/index.html) is another excellent source of free, online tools and information of interest to anyone starting a small business. The "Small Business Planner" section of this site takes you step-by-step through the process of establishing the infrastructure of your new business.

Yet another free, online resource for new business entrepreneurs is the Entrepreneur.com website (entrepreneur.com). This site is maintained by the publisher of *Entrepreneur* magazine and Entrepreneur Press. Click on the "Starting a Business" and "E-Business" icons on the site's homepage to start learning about how to establish your business. The site also offers marketing and advertising tutorials and advice.

What's Next

Once your business's infrastructure is in place, you're ready to start developing your website and marketing your products. The next chapter focuses on how to get your business online in one week or less, and includes information on establishing a basic e-commerce website capable of selling your products.

Chapter 4

Preparing the Website: Assets and Elements You'll Need

*O*K, you're just about ready to start putting together an e-commerce website to sell your product online. This part of the process can, in fact, be completed in a week (or less) once you have all the necessary resources and assets lined up and ready to go.

Because you'll probably be using an e-commerce turnkey solution (at least initially) for your website, you won't be doing

> **WARNING**
>
> Beware of copyright and trademark infringement! Make sure you have
> written permission to use any text, photos, graphics, illustrations, or
> other copyrighted or trademarked materials you plan to use on your website. This applies
> to any material (text, graphics, audio, photographs, videos, animations, logos, etc.) that
> you did not create yourself from scratch and that you do not own the rights to. If you'll
> be using product artwork or product descriptions created by the manufacturer of the prod-
> uct you're selling, for example, make sure you have permission to use these materials
> before incorporating them into your website.

any programming. Instead, you need to select a template that you'll customize during the design phase for your site. The internet service provider you
use for your e-commerce turnkey solution probably has dozens, if not hundreds, of website design templates to choose from.

After choosing a template that offers the overall design and color scheme
you believe best represents your company and its products in cyberspace, you
need to begin customizing it to create your site. To fully customize your site,
there are some important design elements (referred to as *assets*) and website
components that you'll want to create or have created on your behalf. These
assets should be created before you start designing and putting together your
website.

For easy implementation you want to acquire all of your assets in a digital format. For example, all photos, graphics, and illustrations should be created and available to you in a .JPG or .TIF graphic format.

The following are original assets you'll probably want to create (or have
created) for your website:

- *Company logo*. You might consider hiring a professional graphic
  designer to create a professional looking logo for your company.
- *Detailed and professionally-written descriptions of your product*. These
  descriptions should contain no spelling or grammatical errors, be easy
  to read and understand, and provide potential customers with all of
  the information they want or need to know about your product.
- *Website text*. In addition to detailed product descriptions, a well-
  designed and professional-quality website has other text elements to

educate the customer and convey your marketing message. More information about the anatomy of a website is in Chapter 7. However, for planning purposes, additional text elements you might want to add to your website include:

— Company description and background information ("About Us")
— Press releases
— FAQ (frequently-asked questions) documents
— Shipping information
— Product return information
— Customer satisfaction guarantee and customer testimonials
— Contact information
— Website copyright information

➡ *Professional quality photos of your products.* Since people shopping online won't be able touch and feel your product before they make a purchase, it's essential to provide the high-quality photographs. These photos should not only show off your product in the best way possible, they should also showcase details about the product and allow web surfers to see the product from different vantage points, if appropriate.

➡ *Multimedia elements.* If you plan to incorporate animations, audio, or video into your website, you'll want to have these assets created in advance. Adding flashy elements can be a useful marketing tool, as long as what you've added doesn't take away from your overall marketing or sales message.

Creating Your Site's Text

If you have a flare for writing and believe you can write copy that will capture the attention of visitors, effectively communicate your marketing message, and help sell your products online, then by all means you should write your own website copy for the product descriptions and other text elements on your site. It's essential, however, that in addition to being well written, informative, and compelling, all of your text be error free in terms of spelling, punctuation, and grammar.

Because your potential customers will rely on the text on your website, such as your product descriptions, to make their buying decision, seriously consider hiring a professional freelance writer or marketing expert to write your text. A freelance writer, advertising specialist, public relations professional, or marketing expert has the skills and experience necessary to create well-written copy.

You can find freelance writers using a service, such as eLance.com (elance.com), which is ideal for tracking down any type of experienced freelancer, whether it's a photographer, writer, editor, graphic designer, or website programmer. Plan on spending at least several hundred dollars to have a professional writer create product descriptions and other text-based elements. An experience writer will typically charge between $.50 and $1 per word, or quote a flat fee for a specific project. Avoid negotiating an hourly rate for a writer.

Creating Professional Quality Product Photos

How well you depict your product online in terms of the quality of photographs you incorporate into your site will play a tremendous role in building your credibility and generating sales. After all, that timeless saying "A picture is worth a thousand words" definitely holds true. While your text-based product descriptions are important, it's essential that you showcase your products visually using multiple crystal clear, detailed, full-color photographs.

If you're on a tight budget, consider contacting your product's manufacturer or distributor to determine if it already has a selection of quality product images you can incorporate into your site. Another alternative is to contact stock photo agencies to see if you can acquire inexpensive, royalty-free images of your product for your website. To use these images, you'd either pay a fee per image you use or a flat fee to be able to use an unlimited number of images from the stock photo agency's library of images. A typical stock photo agency has a library consisting of hundreds of thousands or even millions of digital images you can download and use instantly. The following are a few agencies worth contacting to obtain stock photographs for your website:

- ➡ http://office.microsoft.com/en-us/clipart/default.aspx
- ➡ adobe.com/products/creativesuite/stockphotos/
- ➡ bigstockphoto.com
- ➡ Comstock.com
- ➡ FotoSearch.com

➡ iStockPhoto.com

➡ Shutterstock.com

Another option is to take your own product images using a high-resolution digital camera in a photo studio you set up in your home. If the product you are photographing is small, you can set up an inexpensive desktop photo studio for a few hundred dollars (plus the price of a camera). For products that are larger, you'll need to use professional-quality lighting and backgrounds to create the images you need.

For professional and amateur photographers alike, the Canon EOS Digital Rebel line of cameras (usa.canon.com/consumer) are ideal for taking product photos to be used on the web. The Digital Rebel XTi, for example, offers 10.1 megapixel resolution and offers three-frames-per-second shooting with virtually no delay. Add a proper background and appropriate lighting, and with a bit of practice, just about anyone can learn to take professional-quality product photographs worthy of being used on any e-commerce website.

For several hundred dollars, you can purchase the lighting and backgrounds needed to take professional-looking product shots. Lighting and background packages can be purchased from companies like Photography Lighting Company (photography-lighting.com) and Amvona (amvona.com). Used or close-out professional photography equipment at discounted prices can be found on eBay.com.

Once you've taken your product photos, you can edit and manipulate them as needed using software, such as Adobe Photoshop Elements, Adobe Photoshop CS3, Apple's iPhoto, or Apple's Aperture. You can then incorporate

---

CLICK TIP

As a general rule, when taking product photographs you want to use a solid color background. Depending on the product and how the photos will be used on your site, a solid white background typically works best. On the other hand, by using photo editing software, such as PhotoShop CS3, you can crop away the background altogether, if desired.

the images into your website. To learn more about Adobe Photoshop, visit the Adobe website (adobe.com).

If you're not interested in becoming your own photographer, but you'd like to incorporate original product photos that you own the rights to on your website, consider hiring a professional photographer to take your product photos for you. You can find local photographers listed in the telephone book or by using a service, such as eLance.com (elance.com), which is ideal for tracking down any type of experienced freelancer, whether it's a photographer, writer, editor, graphic designer, or website programmer. Plan on spending at least several hundred dollars to have a professional photographer create a selection of product images in digital format.

Your Company's Logo

A company logo is typically a graphic image that establishes a visual icon to represent a company. It can be one color or use many colors. A logo can also make use of a specific or custom-designed font or typestyle to spell out your company's name. Having a visually appealing logo helps your company establish credibility and recognition, and it helps set your company apart from its competition.

Once you have a company logo you'll want to showcase it prominently on your website, especially in the masthead area. Additional details about logo placement on a website are found in Chapter 7.

A logo can be created on a computer using graphics software, or it can be hand-drawn by an artist or graphic designer. Ultimately, the logo will need to be transformed into a digital image in order to be incorporated into your website.

Because your logo is an essential part of your company's branding and identity, you want it to look professional, be memorable, and be visually appealing. Ideally, you should hire a graphic artist to help you design your company logo. You can find a professional graphic designer who specializes in freelance logo design using a service like eLance.com. Using any internet search engine, you can also use the search phrase "logo design."

When hiring an artist, make sure he or she is willing to create a handful of potential logo designs for you. You can then narrow down your choices and have one of the designs fine-tuned by the artist to create what you believe is the perfect logo to represent your company. Plan on spending anywhere from $100 to several thousand dollars to have your logo professionally created.

Off-the-shelf logo design software designed for amateurs is available, but the results are typically less professional than if you were to have a professional graphic designer create your logo.

In addition to showcasing your logo on your website, it should also be used on your company letterhead, business cards, and brochures, as well as in your online and print ads. If applicable, it could also be used on your product's packaging.

Your Online Business's URL

After selecting the name of your business, you need to register your website's address, or uniform resource indicator (URL). This process takes just a few minutes and will cost under $10 per URL if you use an internet registrar, such as GoDaddy.com (godaddy.com).

The first step in this process is to brainstorm the perfect website address, aka domain name, for your company. Ideally, the address you select should be easy to remember, easy to spell, and obvious to potential web surfers. For example, if the name of your company is ABC International, you might want your website address to be ABCInternational.com.

Obviously, with so many websites already in existence, many website domain names are already taken. However, with more than 31.7 trillion domain names ending with the .com extension possible, there are still plenty of appealing domain names available.

From a technical standpoint, every website is assigned a unique IP address, which is comprised of a series of numbers between zero and 255. A website's IP address might look like this: 135.52.0.255. To the layperson, this numeric combination means nothing. But to a computer, these numbers are how an internet browser finds your website in the vastness of cyberspace.

Instead of making web surfers memorize a bunch of confusing number combinations for the websites they're looking for, the system of URLs (uniform resource locators) was created. A typical URL has three main components.

The first part typically begins with www. or http://www. The second part is what you actually must select. The third part of a URL is its extension, which is typically .com, however, a variety of other extensions are available, such as .edu, .org, .net., gov, .info, .TV, .biz, .name, and .us. Some of these extensions have specific uses. For example, a website that ends with the extension .gov is typically a government-operated website.

Most web surfers are accustomed to URLs ending with the popular .com extension, so ideally, you want your URL to use it. Potential customers might get confused trying to find your website if it utilizes a less popular extension.

Of course, the same website can have many different URLs that lead to the same place. So, you could potentially register www.abcinternational.com, www.abcinternational.biz, and www.abcinternational.info, to ensure web surfers will be able to find you.

CLICK TIP

In addition to using a search engine to find the websites they're looking for, most web surfers also rely on their common sense. For example, if someone is looking for a company's website, she'll enter "www.[company name].com" on her web browser. Knowing this, you'll want to choose a URL that your potential customers will be able to figure out for themselves (and then remember) using their own common sense.

As you brainstorm the perfect URL, the part of the website address that you create can only use letters, numbers, and the hyphen symbol (-). No other special characters or punctuation marks—such as !, #, $, or ,—can be used. Also, no spaces can be used within a URL. You can use an underscore (_) to represent a space, but this can be confusing to web surfers. Its use is not advisable.

The customizable part of a domain name and the extension (.com, for example) can be up to 63 characters long. As a general rule, the shorter the domain name, the easier it is to remember and type into a web browser accurately. Of course, virtually all of the one, two, three, and four character domain names have long since been taken. Most importantly, the customizable part of the domain name you select must be totally unique and not have already been registered by another person or company. It also may not violate someone else's copyrighted name, company name, or product name.

Domain names are not case sensitive, so you can mix and match upper- and lower-case letters to make a domain name easier to read and promote. For example, you could promote your domain name as www.abccompany.com or www.ABCCompany.com or www.AbcCompany.com.

As you're in the process of brainstorming the perfect domain name for your business, come up with at least five to ten options you like. When you're ready to register your domain name, you first need to determine if the domain name you've selected has already been registered by someone else. This process takes under one minute.

To check if a domain name is registered to someone else, simply go to the website of any domain name registrar, such as GoDaddy.com, Register.com, NetworkSolutions.com, or MyDomain.com, and enter your desired domain name in the field marked "Start a domain search" or "Find a domain name." If the domain name you've entered is available, you will have the opportunity to register it on the spot for an annual fee. If, however, it is already taken, you have three options:

1. You can choose to register an alternative domain name, one that nobody else has.
2. You can contact the person or company that owns the domain name that's taken and offer to purchase or lease it. This typically costs much more than registering a domain name that isn't already taken. Acquiring a domain name from someone else or another company can cost anywhere from under $100 to $1,000,000, depending on the domain name.
3. You can be put on a waiting list and then be notified when and if the domain name you want ever becomes available. The chances of this happening within a reasonable timeframe, however, are relatively slim.

After you've determined that the domain name you want is available, you'll need to register it with an internet domain name registrar. There is an annual fee to register a domain name. Depending on the registrar, registering a single domain name costs between $5.95 and $39.95. Obviously, choose a company with the lowest rates. GoDaddy.com (godaddy.com) tends to offer very competitive rates for domain name registrations, and this company makes the process extremely fast and easy.

Registering your domain name requires you to provide details about yourself and your company, including your name, address, phone number, and credit card information (for paying the annual fee). The process varies based on which domain registrar you use, but it should take no more than five to ten minutes to complete. After you've set up an account, registering additional domain names can be done much faster.

Part of the domain name registration process will most likely involve the need to provide the registrar with your internet service provider's IP address. You may also need to provide what are called DNS numbers to the registrar. This is information that is provided by your internet service provider (ISP), if applicable. Your ISP is the company that will be hosting your website. In this case, it'll probably be the company you select to provide you with an e-commerce turnkey solution.

Ideally, you want your website to have a single domain name that you can promote and that is easy to remember. But, because some people have trouble spelling or get easily confused, you might want to register multiple domain names with slightly different spellings. This way, if someone accidentally types the wrong domain name into his web browser, he'll still wind up at your website. Think about some of the common typos or ways people might misspell your domain name, and register those as well.

Also, to ensure you generate the most traffic possible to your website, consider registering domain names that relate to the product you'll be selling. Think about the search phrases, keywords, or terms someone might use who is looking for your product online, and incorporate those terms into your domain name. That way, if someone is looking for a widget and she types "www.widget.com" into her browser, she'll find your website. Be creative as you register your domain names, keeping in mind that it's perfectly OK to have ten or more domain names ending up at the same website.

Putting the Pieces Together

This chapter has focused on some of the assets and elements you'll need to create a professional-looking website to sell your products. Now that you have the various pieces to your website's puzzle, it's time to put those pieces together to create the most effective website possible—one that's designed to effectively sell your products!

Before proceeding, make sure you have the following assets and elements ready to incorporate into your website:

➡ Company logo
➡ Product descriptions
➡ Product photographs and illustrations

➡ Additional text elements for your site (company background, FAQs, return policy, guarantee, testimonials, etc.)

➡ Any multimedia content you plan to add to your site (audio, video, animations, etc.)

➡ Your registered website domain name(s)

What's Next

The next several chapters focus on the complete turnkey solutions available from a variety of different companies that allows you to take a generic website template and transform it (using the assets and elements you've already created) into a fully customized website specifically to promote and sell your products.

This part of the website design and publishing process can be done relatively easily, quickly, and inexpensively. However, the more creative you are at making your website easy to use, unique, and functional, the easier it will be for you to attract traffic to your site and transform those web surfers into paying customers. Remember, the focus of your site should be to sell your product—not show off flashy online bells and whistles.

Chapter 5

An Introduction to E-Commerce Turnkey Solutions

*O*nline sales are expected to hit $144 billion per year by 2010. Using an e-commerce turnkey solution, getting in on this potential moneymaking opportunity has never been easier. And as you're about to discover, your initial investment can be as low as a few hundred dollars.

Thus far, you've been reading about how e-commerce turnkey solutions offered by a variety of companies can be an ideal solution for helping you launch your e-commerce website quickly, easily, and with absolutely no programming required. In fact, with many of these solutions, you can have a website up and running in less than one week.

Instead of having to hire a team of programmers to design and launch a website from scratch (which would take weeks or months to create and cost you thousands, if not tens of thousands of dollars in development costs), an e-commerce turnkey solution provides you with a selection of professional-looking website templates that you can fully customize.

Each template includes the components needed to create a highly functional e-commerce website capable of handling secure transactions. In addition, website hosting services and the ability to accept major credit cards and other online payment options are available (for an additional fee), so you may not need to acquire a separate merchant account.

While the website templates available to you may not offer all of the flashy design elements you might like to incorporate into your site, they do offer the core functionality necessary to launch your e-commerce business and to test its viability. Once your business is successful, you should definitely plan on expanding and fine-tuning the website on an ongoing basis.

The Pros and Cons of Using This Solution

The main reasons to go with an e-commerce turnkey solution to launch your online venture are the time and money you'll save. Many of the companies that offer these turnkey solutions have created an entire suite of easy-to-use online tools to assist you in designing, creating, launching, and then managing your business.

Some of the biggest benefits of using a turnkey solution for your e-commerce website are

- ➡ low startup cost.
- ➡ one company provides the development tools for the website itself and secure website hosting services. For an additional fee, the same company will allow you to accept multiple forms of online payments, including major credit cards, electronic checks, Google Checkout, and/or PayPal's Express Checkout.
- ➡ that absolutely no programming is required.
- ➡ the ability to design and launch a basic site in less than one week.

➡ the ability to choose from dozens or even hundreds of professional-looking website templates and then customize your favorite to give your site a unique look.

➡ that by using the same suite of online tools, you can design, publish, maintain, and promote your site, and track traffic to the site and synchronize sales data to financial software applications, such as Intuit Software's QuickBooks, to better handle your record keeping and accounting. Many of the turnkey solutions also offer modules for maintaining a customer database, managing inventory, and keeping detailed order shipment records (including the ability to print shipping labels and track packages shipped via the U.S. Postal Service, FedEx, UPS, or DHL).

You'll also discover that usually several different e-commerce turnkey solution options are available from each company. Each package comes with a slightly different selection of tools and resources, at different price points, so you don't have to overspend in order to launch your business.

For example, GoDaddy.com is a well-established company that offers a vast selection of easy-to-use, online tools and resources designed to make creating and launching an e-commerce website fast and easy. If you'll be initially selling no more than 20 different products, GoDaddy's Quick Shopping Cart Economy Edition ($6.99 to $9.99 per month) offers the tools you need to create an online store showcasing up to 20 products. You'll also be able to accept PayPal an as online payment method.

GoDaddy.com's Quick Shopping Cart Deluxe Edition ($20.99 to $29.99 per month) offers additional website creation tools and features, including the ability to showcase and sell up to 100 products from your site. The Quick Shopping Cart Premium Edition ($34.99 to $49.99 per month) allows you to showcase and sell an unlimited number of products.

Website hosting, online security (including the ability to create an SSL-enabled site) is included with each Quick Shopping Cart package. Chapter 6 offers more information about how to launch your website using GoDaddy's Quick Shopping Cart turnkey solutions. You'll learn more about the online security measures that are essential for any e-commerce website later in this chapter. See the Security Considerations section.

The eBay Stores (http://stores.ebay.com) and eBay ProStores (pro stores.com) sites offer distinct business models and several different service tiers or packages for online merchants. Each of these packages comes with the tools to build your store using templates that can be customized in more than 300 ways. The tools to then promote your store, manage sales, and track your success are also included. Chapter 6 covers using eBay Stores or ProStores to launch your online-based venture.

The various turnkey based solutions are ideal for startup businesses. However, as your online venture grows, you may want to add website functionality that might not be available from the e-commerce turnkey solution provider you choose. Thus, as you shop around for a service provider, look for one that allows you to expand and grow your website over time so you can add functionality as it becomes necessary.

CLICK TIP

Before you start creating your website, whether it's from scratch or by customizing a template, spend time surfing the web looking for other sites that you consider to be well-designed and that you'd like yours to emulate. Determine in advance what features and functionality you are likely to want as well as what design elements you'd like to incorporate into your site. Knowing your immediate needs and what your needs might be in the future will help you choose a turnkey solution that's best suited for your business venture.

One of the big drawbacks many turnkey solutions have is that the design capabilities and functionality you'll be able to offer on your site are ultimately limited by what's offered by the turnkey solution provider you opt to deal with. For example, you may be limited in terms of how much you can actually customize a template in terms of its look or functionality. At some point, you may outgrow what the service provider is capable of offering.

Thus down the road, you may find it necessary to pursue different options, such as having a website created from scratch or hiring your own programmers to further customize the website template you're utilizing. Some online business operators find that the biggest drawback of using a turnkey solution is that it limits their ability to grow and expand the functionality of the site in the future.

Initial Startup Costs

The initial startup costs of launching your business will vary greatly based on a number of factors. They include:

➡ the cost of your inventory;

➡ how much advertising and marketing you plan to do;

➡ the decisions made when setting up the infrastructure for your business venture (discussed in Chapter 3);

➡ how much you spend creating original assets, such as logos, custom photography, and animations for your website; and

➡ which e-commerce turnkey solution you use to create and launch your online business.

In the past, creating and hosting a secure website capable of handling online financial transactions (processing credit card orders, for example), was usually the most costly aspect of launching an online business. Today, thanks to the turnkey solutions discussed in this chapter and Chapter 6, it's become an extremely inexpensive as well as a very straightforward process.

What you'll need to really focus on (and invest time and money in) is properly marketing and advertising your new business in order to generate ongoing traffic to the website. Without visitors to your website, you'll receive no orders. A lack of orders translates into zero revenue and potential financial losses.

A big challenge startup online business owners face is generating traffic to their new website and setting their online business apart from their competition. Those who do this successfully have a much greater chance of success. In most cases, generating traffic and buyers requires making a significant financial investment in advertising, marketing, public relations, and promotions—all of which need to be geared specifically to your business's primary target audience.

Chapter 9 focuses on successful marketing, advertising, public relations, and marketing strategies. If you choose to handle this yourself and take a grassroots approach, and capitalize on word-of-mouth advertising, your investment can be significantly lower than if you hire an advertising and/or public relations agency (or freelance marketing experts) to design and launch a multifaceted campaign on a regional or national level.

One mistake many first-time businesspeople make is investing a large budget in advertising and marketing, for example, but using that money ineffectively by designing a poorly-conceived campaign targeted to the wrong audience.

Spending a fortune on advertising and marketing doesn't guarantee you success. It greatly increases your chances of success, however, if the money you invest is spent properly on designing highly effective ads and then placing those ads in media that your target audience are exposed to. Advertising, marketing, public relations, and promotions are all skills that people spend years fine-tuning. If you don't possess these skills, seriously consider hiring professionals who can generate much better results from your advertising/marketing budget than you.

As you calculate your startup budget, you want to allocate as much money as possible for designing and launching the most professional and easy-to-use website possible, as well as for properly marketing the site in order to generate traffic to it. Simply publishing a website on the internet and registering it with the search engines and web directories, such as Google and Yahoo!, is not enough. (It is, however, an important start, as you'll discover in Chapter 10.)

Part of the business plan you create should include detailed financial forecasts that list all of your startup costs and the costs of operating your business during the first few weeks or months until it becomes profitable.

Understanding Online Payment Options

When it comes to starting an online business, one of the most important steps is figuring out how people will pay for their orders. You must decide if you'll accept major credit cards, electronic checks, PayPal, or Google

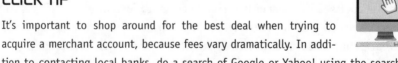

CLICK TIP

It's important to shop around for the best deal when trying to acquire a merchant account, because fees vary dramatically. In addition to contacting local banks, do a search of Google or Yahoo! using the search phrase "Merchant Account." You should also contact your website hosting company because most already have partnerships with merchant account providers, which makes it easier for you to get started accepting credit card payments.

Checkout. Your goal should be to be able to accept orders quickly, easily, and securely from the largest group of people possible, which typically means being able to accept Visa, MasterCard, Discover, and American Express.

The ability to accept credit card payments requires you, the business operator, to acquire a *merchant account* through a bank or financial

CLICK TIP

One reason to accept credit cards is to provide convenience to your customers. Studies have shown that consumers are apt to spend more on purchases when using a major credit card (as opposed to writing a check or paying cash, for example).

institution. This typically means paying an application fee, filling out paperwork, and then paying a per-transaction fee, plus a small percentage of each credit card sale to the merchant account provider. Your merchant account provider must also provide resources that are compatible with your website hosting company so credit card orders can be processed securely and in real time online.

By depending on the e-commerce turnkey solution provider you work with, you may be able to simply pay extra fees to add credit card processing capabilities to your website. For example, GoDaddy.com offers merchant accounts in conjunction with its website packages for an added $59.95 application fee, $20

CLICK TIP

Because you're operating an online business, not a traditional retail business, when you apply for a credit card merchant account, you will need a Mail Order/Telephone Order (MOTO) or Card Not Present account. You require the ability to process someone's credit card information without physically swiping a card to complete the transaction. Theoretically, this increases the possibility of fraud, which means you'll probably wind up paying higher rates to accept credit card transactions than would a traditional retail business. To process your credit/debit card orders, you'll ultimately need a merchant account and a virtual terminal or gateway (provided or set up by the merchant account provider). The virtual terminal/gateway connects your website to the credit card processing company so your transactions can be approved and completed in real time online.

CLICK TIP

Most merchant account providers can set you up with the capacity to accept Visa, MasterCard, Discover, and American Express payments, as well as debit card payments and electronic check payments. The fees, however, may be different for each credit card or payment type. For example, depending on the merchant account provider, you may wind up paying a higher per-transaction fee and/or discount rate for an order paid for using an American Express card or an electronic check.

monthly fee, a $.35 per transaction fee, and a 2.59 percent fee per transaction (based on the total order). Whatever fees you wind up paying to accept credit card payments must be figured in your cost of doing business. It may be necessary to forward some of these costs on to your customers by raising your retail prices slightly for the products you'll be selling.

To be competitive selling products in cyberspace, it's absolutely essential that your business be able to accept credit card and debit card payments. Being able to accept electronic checks is also an added service you might opt to extend to your customers.

The following are five strategies for obtaining a merchant account:

1. Compare prices carefully and watch out for hidden and recurring fees. Most merchant account providers charge a percentage of each sale (called the *discount rate*) in addition to a fixed per-transaction fee. Additional fees you'll want to compare are the application fees for setting up the account and any recurring monthly fee you're required to pay in order to maintain the account and be able to accept credit card payments. You may be offered a lower discount rate by one provider but a higher per-transaction fee, or a higher than average recurring monthly fee. Other potential fees to watch out for are associated with having to purchase or lease credit card processing equipment and/or software.

2. For a startup company with no sales track record, negotiating for lower rates from a merchant account provider is a challenge. However, once you develop a relationship with your merchant account provider and demonstrate a track record of growing monthly sales, you could go back and try to negotiate a lower per-transaction fee and/or discount rate. Even a small reduction to your discount rate

will save you a fortune over time and instantly increase your profit margin on whatever you're selling.

3. The contract you're required to sign with your merchant account provider is usually complex and confusing legal document. Before signing it, understand exactly what you're agreeing to in terms of the fees and the duration of the contract. If you sign a two-year agreement, for example, but your business only remains open for six months, you're still required to pay the minimum monthly fees for the duration of the contracted agreement (or pay a hefty cancellation fee).

4. Make sure the merchant account provider you choose offers the tools and resources necessary to seamlessly integrate credit card processing into your website (through your website hosting service). A lack of compatibility causes tremendous headaches and costs you extra getting everything to work properly. Ease of implementation as well as security are important factors to consider.

5. Not all merchant account providers are alike. In addition to charging different fees, each offers its own level of customer service and technical support. You need to know how quickly transactions are processed and when the money from incoming credit card sales gets automatically deposited in your company's bank account. How long this takes (between a few hours and several days) varies among merchant account providers. Many providers also offer lower rates and fees to low-risk businesses. Operating an escort business, online poker site, or credit restoration business, for example, is regarded as high-risk.

PayPal (800-514-4920, paypal.com) or Google Checkout (checkout .google.com) are online payment options that are easy for online business operators to register for. These services allow registered members to pay for their purchases using a major credit card, debit card or electronic check. However, only accepting these forms of payment, instead of major credit cards, restricts your potential customer base to only those web savvy shoppers who are members of the PayPal or Google Checkout services.

PayPal, for example, boasts more than 150 million members worldwide and allows website operators to add an express checkout feature onto their sites, which can speed up the process of placing an order for your customers.

You can learn more about how to accept PayPal or Google Checkout payments on your site and the fees associated with these services in Chapter 8.

Security Considerations

Perhaps the biggest concern among consumers shopping online is the possibility of credit card fraud and identity theft. If a consumer visits your website and doesn't feel safe making a purchase, he'll wind up shopping elsewhere.

How you design your website and position your company contributes to its perceived credibility among people visiting your website for the first time. However, when it comes right down to it, in addition to showcasing yourself as a reliable, trustworthy, and legitimate business, you also need to put proper online security measures in place to protect your business as well as your customers.

Your website hosting service, e-commerce turnkey solution provider, and/or your credit card merchant account provider can assist you in incorporating adequate online security measures onto your website in order to prevent credit card fraud and other security-related problems. Although you can cut corners and eliminate some of these security precautions, doing so opens you up to legal problems and decreases your credibility among potential customers.

For an e-commerce website to be considered safe and secure, it needs to offer secure transactions using the secure electronic transaction protocol (SET), the secure sockets layer (SSL) protocol, or another form of encryption and online security that allows you (the online merchant) to accept and process credit card information and personal data from your clients without that data being compromised or inadvertently made available to the general public or hackers. Assuming you're using a turnkey solution to host your website, chances are that all of the necessary security is either already built in or available at an additional fee.

VeriSign is the leading source for secure sockets layer (SSL) certificate authority, which enables secure e-commerce and communications for websites, intranets, and extranets. The company secures more than 500,000 web servers worldwide with strong encryption and rigorous authentication.

According to VeriSign, "Without SSL encryption, packets of information travel through networks in full view. Imagine sending mail through the postal system in a clear envelope. Anyone with access to it can see the data. If it looks valuable, they might take it or change it. Without third-party verification, how do you know a website is really a business you trust? Imagine receiving an envelope with no return address and a form asking for your bank account number. An SSL certificate helps website visitors protect sensitive information and get a better idea of who they are trusting with it."

As an online merchant, SSL helps you deliver a secure and convenient way for customers to interact with you over the internet. The company reports that, "VeriSign is the SSL Certificate provider of choice for over 93 percent of the Fortune 500 and the world's 40 largest banks." As an online merchant, by displaying the VeriSign Secured Seal on your site (near the online order form or shopping cart), your customers will recognize the most trusted security mark on the internet.

CLICK TIP

To learn more about online security relating to credit card transactions, call (866) 893-6565, or visit the VeriSign website (verisign.com/ssl/ssl-information-center/index.html).

Selecting the Right E-Commerce Turnkey Solution

Every online business has different needs, based on what's being sold, to whom products are being sold, and what features and functionality the online merchant wishes to incorporate into her e-commerce site. Once you pinpoint what you want and need, finding a complete turnkey solution that meets your requirements at a price you can afford is a relatively straightforward process.

CLICK TIP

In addition to the core functionality you want and need to operate your e-commerce website, some turnkey solutions offer the ability to automatically or easily list your items for sale through online auction sites, such as eBay.com. For startup online entrepreneurs, offering products on eBay.com, for example, can be way to promote a new business, test market new products, and generate additional revenue. If your turnkey solution provider offers an eBay listing tool, for example, this could save you time and effort listing and managing online auctions for your products. Likewise, if you plan to use QuickBooks to manage your business's finances, seamless integration between your turnkey solution and this software is beneficial.

As you look at what each e-commerce turnkey solution offers, don't just look at a list of features and make your decision. Be sure to visit several e-commerce websites that currently utilize the services of the company you're thinking about working with, and invest time exploring those websites. Considering how your own site will be customized, do the sites you're looking at offer the professional look, functionality, and user interface that could work well for your business? Will you be able to easily customize the templates to create a site you're proud of and that meets your needs? Ultimately, choosing the best turnkey solution to meet the needs of your unique online business could mean the difference between success and failure.

CLICK TIP

Listing your products on services such as Google Product Search (google.com/base/help/sellongoogle.html) and/or price comparison websites, such as Nextag.com (http://merchants.nextag.com/serv/main/advertise/Advertise.do) can also be useful marketing tools. Google AdWords, Yahoo Small Business, and Microsoft adCenter are also services that can be used to promote your business (see Chapter 10). Some turnkey solutions make using these services to promote your products a seamless process that ties directly to the management tools used to operate your e-commerce website.

Chapter 6 offers details about some of the most popular complete turnkey solutions available to online business operators looking to get their e-commerce websites up and running quickly and inexpensively. Beyond the turnkey solutions described in this book, however, you can find additional options using any internet search engine and entering the search phrase "e-commerce website," "e-commerce website creation," or "online business creation." You can also find ads for these services in popular computer magazines and publications, such as *Entrepreneur* magazine, that target small business operators and entrepreneurs.

What's Next

Now that you have a basic idea of what to expect from a complete e-commerce turnkey solution, the next chapter provides detailed information about some of the specific services available to merchants. Chapter 7 then discusses e-commerce website design fundamentals. The information offered in these chapters will help you create the most easy-to-use, visually pleasing, credible, user-friendly, and professional-looking site possible, and allow you to incorporate the elements needed to convince potential customers to confidently place their order online via your site.

Chapter 6

E-Commerce Turnkey Solution Round-Up

*U*tilizing a complete e-commerce turnkey solution to design, launch, and operate your online business offers a wide range of benefits:

- ➡ No programming is required.
- ➡ Startup costs are very low.
- ➡ Your site can be designed and launched in less than one week.

- Using a template provided by the turnkey solution provider, it's easy to make your site look professional and offer the functionality required to make it easy to use for your visitors.
- The turnkey solution providers offer all of the tools needed to design, launch, and operate your online business for one monthly fee.

This chapter provides details about some of the most popular complete e-commerce turnkey solutions available from well-known providers, such as eBay.com, GoDaddy.com, Network Solutions, and Yahoo!. The companies and the products described here, however, are only a small sampling of the e-commerce solutions available to startup online business owners.

Shopping for Your E-Commerce Turnkey Solution

As you formulate the idea for your online business and determine the functionality you require from your site, you want to look closely at the turnkey offerings to find a solution that's best suited for your business concept. In addition to comparing the startup costs and ongoing monthly fees associated with each service, you also want to evaluate the

- tools and resources offered by the service provider.
- professional quality and selection of the site templates being offered.
- ease of use of the website design tools and other resources offered to help operate your business.
- technical support services provided.
- e-commerce functions that can be easily incorporated into your website using the development tools provided.
- ability to accept and process online payments from customers.
- online security measures your site will be able to incorporate.
- resources offered to help you market and promote your online business
- ability to integrate easily your site's order and customer data with your accounting, spreadsheet, and/or order management software.
- ease of use, functionality, and professional appearance of the shopping cart module that will be incorporated into your site using the turnkey solution you select.
- extra fees or hidden charges you'll be responsible for in order to get your website designed, launched, and operational.

➡ expandability of your site in the future, using compatible third-party tools and resources.

Now that you know what you're looking for from an e-commerce turnkey solution, the rest of this chapter focuses on describing a handful of your possible options. The services described in this chapter were selected because of their features and functionality, competitive pricing, and the fact that they're being offered by well-established, highly reputable service providers.

> **CLICK TIP**
>
> To find additional companies offering similar solutions using an internet search engine, such as Yahoo! or Google, enter a search phrase, such as, "e-commerce turnkey solution," "e-commerce solutions," "website creation solutions," or "web store development."

eBay Stores

Service provider: eBay.com

Website: http://pages.ebay.com/storefronts/start.html

Turnkey solution pricing: $15.95 to $299.95 per month

The folks at the online auction site, eBay have devised a way for sellers to take full advantage of the eBay auction sales model and also sell their products online using more traditional fixed-price methods. The result is eBay Stores (not to be confused with eBay ProStores, which are described later in the chapter).

For merchants, monthly fees start at $15.95 for a Basic Store, $49.95 for a Premium Store, or $299.95 for an Anchor Store. Once you choose which tier is most suitable for your needs as an online seller, you're provided with a roster of online tools to help you design and manage your store. In addition to these recurring monthly charges, eBay Stores also charges its merchants listing fees.

If you're looking to create an extremely professional online presence but don't have the experience or expertise to do this, eBay will put you in contact with a Certified eBay Stores Designer, who for an additional fee will help you design and launch your eBay Store. However, using eBay's Quick Store Set-Up module, you can customize a template and have a basic store up and running within a few hours.

Using a template, you can add your company's logo and store description; incorporate product photos for what you'll be selling and corresponding text-based product descriptions; divide your products up by categories to make them easy to find by customers; add a navigational toolbar to your main page; showcase specific products, sales, or promotions on your main page; plus add a variety of other features designed to make your customers' shopping experience efficient and your store a welcoming place to visit.

In fact, using one of the eBay Stores templates, you can customize up to 300 different elements of each template in order to create a unique shopping experience for your customers. Once your online store is designed and launched, the eBay Stores turnkey solution offers a variety of tools to help you market and promote your business and drive traffic to your site.

If you plan to get started selling between 10 and 49 items and expect to generate at least $100 in sales per month, the Basic Store is the perfect entry-level option. If you plan to sell more than 50 different products and/or generate at least $500 per month in sales, the Premium Store package is probably more suitable. The Anchor Store option is most suited to high-volume merchants looking for the maximum amount of exposure.

Because eBay Stores utilizes the online auction model, additional product listing fees apply. You do, however, save money on your listing fees as a eBay Stores operator compared to an individual posting single items. As an eBay Stores operator, you're also responsible for other fees, based on the tools and resources you use to promote and operate your store and the eBay Stores tier you sign up for.

To preview what an eBay Store can look like and see some of the functionality that can be built into an online business using this particular turnkey solution, visit the eBay Stores Design Center (http://pages.ebay.com/storefronts/designcenter.html). You can learn strategies for success using this turnkey solution from the free online eBay Stores Tutorials (http://pages.ebay.com/storefronts/tutorials.html) and read success stories from fellow online merchants who currently use eBay Stores (http://pages.ebay.com/storefronts/success.html).

If your online business can benefit from customers being able to click on Buy It Now in order to immediately purchase your products at the fixed price points you set and you'd also like to sell your products by making them available through online auctions, the eBay Stores complete turnkey solution may be suitable for your online business.

According to eBay, within the eBay environment where millions of online auctions take place every day, eBay Stores offers, "a comprehensive eCommerce solution that helps you get more out of eBay's access to millions of shoppers worldwide. By showcasing all of your merchandise in one central location, an eBay Store creates a shopping destination where buyers can learn more about you, your products and your policies."

Furthermore, eBay reports that, "75 percent of eBay Stores sellers surveyed said that opening an eBay Store increased their sales. eBay Stores makes sellers successful by providing powerful tools to help sellers build, manage, promote, and track their eBay presence. We have found that higher volume and more experienced sellers who are committed to growing their sales and expect to have a part-time or full-time business on eBay tend to get the best results from their eBay Stores."

To open an eBay Store, you must have an active eBay account with a Feedback score of 20 or higher. You must also have your ID verified by eBay and have a PayPal account in good standing. The majority of your financial transactions related to your online sales generated will be handled through PayPal. This allows customers who have a PayPal account to make purchases using a major credit card, debit card, or electronic check, or transfer funds held in their pre-existing PayPal account.

The eBay Stores turnkey solution offers a comprehensive collection of tools to create, launch, and manage an online business, and takes full advantage of eBay's online auctions business model. It may or may not be suitable for your particular business venture, based on your unique goals and objectives.

eBay ProStores

Service provider: eBay.com

Phone number: (866) 747-3229

Website: prostores.com

Turnkey solution pricing: $6.95 to $249.95 per month, plus additional fees

Unlike eBay Stores, which uses the online auction model to allow merchants to sell their products, eBay's ProStores offers a complete solution for operating a more traditional e-commerce website, complete with Shopping Cart module.

As a complete solution, ProStores provides tools to handle everything from website development to inventory management and merchandising. For people first getting started and looking to test their online business idea, the ProStores Express service starts at just $6.95 per month, and it also charges a 1.5 percent per transaction fee on every sale. The Express service allows you to design a basic e-commerce website and get it up and running within a few hours, provided you'll be selling fewer than ten products.

For online business operators with more advanced and extensive needs, eBay offers ProStores Business, ProStores Advanced, and ProStores Enterprise ($29.95, $74.95, and $249.95 per month respectively, with a $.50 per transaction fee). With these different plans, online businesses can grow almost limitlessly as needed.

ProStores works seamlessly with eBay Stores and traditional eBay auctions, so merchants can also take advantage of online auctions to sell products. However, the goal of ProStores, like Yahoo! Stores (described later in the chapter), is to provide all the tools an online business operator needs, without requiring them to have any programming or website design skills or experience. All websites are created by fully customizing templates. ProStores, however, offers extreme flexibility when it comes to utilizing these templates, so if you do have programming skills (or wish to hire a programmer to modify your site), it's certainly possible.

If your website design needs exceed the capability that the online tools are capable of, ProStores offers a team of professional website designers who for an additional fee can create e-commerce sites from scratch or add full customization to existing templates. A fully functional e-commerce site can be created for a one-time fee of $399 to $649, depending on the site development package you purchase.

For example, the $649 website design package fully utilizes all of ProStore's capabilities and includes a customized version of the following web pages: Homepage, About Us, Customer Service, Store Location(s), Privacy Policy, FAQs, Store Policies, an online catalog featuring up to 20 products (adding additional products costs $20 each or you can do it yourself for free), a fully integrated shopping cart module, plus PayPal and/or online credit card processing functionality (with basic shipping and sales tax calculations). For an additional fee, ProStores will even maintain your site and keep it updated with new content that you provide.

Of course, if you don't wish to use ProStores professionals to design and maintain your website, you can use the online tools provided to do everything yourself or hire your own team of freelance professionals.

According to eBay, "ProStores offers a fully-featured Web store that can be customized specifically for each online seller. Unlike an eBay Store, ProStores sites are accessed through a URL unique to the seller and have no eBay branding. ProStores sellers are also responsible for driving their own traffic. While items on ProStores sites will sell at fixed prices only, they can also be easily listed onto the eBay Marketplace in either the auction or fixed price formats."

ProStores Business and service tiers above are fully integrated with many popular online payment gateways and merchant account providers, which means no additional software is required for your online store to accept and process credit card payments with your own merchant account. Some of the merchant account providers ProStores is fully compatible with include: Authorize.net (authorize.net), CyberSource (cybersource.com), Innovative Gateway Solutions (innovativegateway.com), LinkPoint (linkpoint.com), Payflow Pro (paypal.com), and QuickBooks Merchant Services (quickbooks merchantservice.com).

From a bookkeeping and client database management standpoint, ProStores is compatible with several third-party software packages, including QuickBooks from Intuit (quickbooks.com). A variety of online marketing, advertising, and promotional tools is also available.

For startup online businesses and business operators first learning about e-commerce, ProStores offers technical support, easy-to-use tutorials, and a comprehensive set of online tools to handle virtually all aspects of getting your business venture designed, launched, and fully operational. This turnkey solution is ideal for people with little or no programming knowledge. To see several fully operational eCommerce websites that utilize eBay ProStores, visit prostores.com/prostores-featured.shtml.

FatCow.com

Service provider: FatCow
Phone number: (866) 544-9343

Website: fatcow.com

Turnkey solution pricing: $29.95 to $49.95 per month, plus additional fees

Virtually every internet service provider (ISP) in the world offering website hosting also offers tools to its customers for creating and launching an e-commerce website. Fatcow.com is no exception. In addition to providing basic website hosting for as little as $88 per year, this company also offers an inexpensive and easy-to-use e-commerce turnkey solution that allows credit card processing (for an additional fee), plus the tools necessary to build a basic, no-frills (but professional looking) e-commerce website quickly and inexpensively.

The ShopSite Manager toolkit, priced at $29.95 per month, allows you to develop an online store with an unlimited number of products. The ShopSite Pro service ($49.95 per month) offers additional features to make it easier to showcase products within your store, customize the site templates, and market your products. For someone planning to sell fewer than 15 products, the ShopSite Starter plan (included with basic website hosting services) is an ideal starting option.

All e-commerce sites created using ShopSite offer PayPal and Google Checkout compatibility (see Chapter 8). For an additional fee, you can obtain your own credit card merchant account and process real-time credit card transactions. To obtain a merchant account through FatCow.com (which ensures compatibility with your site), there is an additional fee of $19.95 per month, a fee of 2.19 percent of each total sale, and $.25 per transaction fee. A $25 monthly processing minimum also applies.

As you'd expect from a complete e-commerce turnkey solution, ShopSite requires absolutely no programming knowledge. A basic e-commerce website can be created and launched in just hours—not days or weeks. All of the tools needed to design, launch, and manage your site are online, so there's no need to purchase and install any specialized software for your computer.

To see a sampling of demo stores created using ShopSite, visit shopsite.com/demo.html. Fatcow, a website hosting and e-commerce turnkey solution provider, has been in business since 1998. According to the company's website, "We took a look around and saw lots of techno babble, confusing pricing schemes, and not much in the way of customer satisfaction or support. We decided that a simpler, more customer-friendly approach was needed . . . We've grown our company with a dedicated group of talented believers in the notion that simple, old-fashioned service and value still ring true."

GoDaddy.com's WebSite Tonight and Quick Shopping Cart

Service provider: GoDaddy

Website: godaddy.com

Turnkey solution pricing: $9.95 to $49.99 per month (plus additional fees)

In addition to being a well-established website hosting service and ISP, GoDaddy.com is also an inexpensive domain name registrar and offers a wide range of à la carte online tools for promoting and managing any type of website. For people interested in launching an online business that utilizes an e-commerce site (complete with shopping cart module), GoDaddy's turnkey solution is Quick Shopping Cart.

By default, the Quick Shopping Cart application can be fully customized and is compatible with PayPal and some independent credit card merchant accounts. For an additional fee, an online business operator can, however, obtain a merchant account through GoDaddy, which allows for secure, real-time credit card transactions.

The Economy Quick Shopping Cart application ($9.99 per month), which can be used to create a stand-alone e-commerce site or incorporated seamlessly into any website, allows a product catalog of up to 20 items. The plan includes 50 megabytes of online storage, plus one gigabyte of monthly bandwidth. The Deluxe Quick Shopping Cart ($29.00 per month) allows a product catalog with up to 100 items, including one gigabyte of online storage plus 50 gigabytes of bandwidth per month. In addition, the application can be integrated with QuickBooks.

For an online businessperson with a large selection of items and plans to expand her offerings over time, GoDaddy's Premium Edition Quick Shopping Cart ($49.99 per month) allows an unlimited products catalog, includes two gigabytes of online storage and 100 gigabytes per month of bandwidth, and has QuickBooks integration.

GoDaddy's Quick Shopping Cart allows secure online transactions and offers a variety of tools to customize the shoppers' experiences when they visit your site. The comprehensive selection of tools also allows you to properly manage your online business, track orders, and market your business. Using this service, you design the look of your store, add products to your catalog, and select shipping, payment, and tax options.

GoDaddy.com offers a menu of fee-based services for the e-commerce business operator, including basic website hosting and domain name registration. For low additional fees (charged monthly or annually), a shopping cart/e-commerce module (called Quick Shopping Cart) can be added to any website. You can also obtain a credit card merchant account through GoDaddy.com, and use the company's Traffic Blazer Plus service to kick off your search engine listing and optimization efforts and begin promoting your business.

GoDaddy.com has also bundled its online tools into a package designed specifically for e-commerce entrepreneurs. You can add to this bundle, however, by paying for additional services separately. For example, website hosting, combined with GoDaddy.com's Website Tonight website development tools, and the Economy Quick Shopping Cart are available as a bundle for an annual fee starting at just $155.54 per year.

There are several different options for establishing your own credit card merchant account through GoDaddy. A Standard Merchant Account allows you to accept orders from the United States only. There's a one-time application fee of $59.95, a monthly fee of $20, a Discount Rate of 2.59 percent per transaction and a per-transaction fee of $.35.

Depending on what you're selling and if you want to accept orders from the United States and Canada, you may need to apply for a Specialty Merchant Account. The application fee is $199. There's also a $20 monthly fee, a discount rate of 2.39 percent per transaction, and a per-transaction fee of $.30.

An International Merchant Account allows you to accept and process credit card orders from virtually anywhere in the world. There's a $695 application fee, a $20 per month fee, a discount rate that starts at 4.95 percent per transaction, and a $.40 per-transaction fee.

Merchants receive the funds from credit card orders within 24 to 72 hours, and applications for merchant accounts are typically approved within one day. The merchant account you acquire through GoDaddy works seamlessly with the WebSite Tonight and Quick Shopping Cart applications and allows for secure online payment transactions.

Another nice feature of the Quick Shopping Cart application is that merchants can quickly sell items through eBay auctions (using a special Certified eBay listing tool). GoDaddy offers telephone and online technical support 24 hours per day, seven days per week. Overall, this is one of the more robust and flexible e-commerce turnkey solutions available. And the services are offered at very competitive prices and are easy to use, with no programming required.

1&1 eShops

Service provider: 1&1 Internet Inc.

Phone number: (877) GO-1AND1

Website: http://order.1and1.com/xml/order/Eshops

Turnkey solution pricing: $5 to $25 per month (plus additional fees)

After recently celebrating its 20th anniversary in business (an extremely impressive achievement for any internet company), 1&1 Internet Inc. now boasts that it is the world's largest website hosting service. As such, it offers a variety of site hosting and development tools, as well as its powerful yet extremely inexpensive eShops service—a turnkey solution for developing an e-commerce site quickly and inexpensively.

Using the eShops online development tools, merchants can quickly and easily customize site templates to give their online store a unique but professional look and design. For someone with a bit more experience, a completely original design, without using a template, can also be created.

Starting at just $5 per month for a basic eShop capable of selling up to 50 different products, this is an excellent deal for someone getting started with an online business venture. Without possessing a merchant account, online payments through PayPal can automatically be utilized by your eShop site. You can, however, also incorporate real-time credit card processing if you have your own merchant account.

According to the company, "1&1 provides a complete online store with no installation necessary. Build your eCommerce website with ease using our eShops. You can choose from more than 30 customizable, ready-to-go templates. We include a choice of payment/shipping methods, customer/invoice numbers and e-mail order confirmation. You also have the ability to check and administer your 1&1 eShop from anywhere and at any time . . . . You don't have to install anything because the shop software will automatically be set up for you. Depending on the particular package, each shop has a certain amount of disk space. Although a small part of this already has been used for the shop software, most of it is available for your data. There will be regular backups of your shop . . . . Your eShop can be set up step-by-step. There are several set-up wizards presented as pop-up windows, for basic settings, payment methods, shipping methods, etc. You can decide how the shipping costs should be calculated for each shipping method by setting a minimum shipping charge of your choice, and set different rates based on the total order amount . . . . Like the Control Panel, the eShop Administration pages are SSL encrypted. So confidential information, such as order book and customer administration, cannot be accessed by third parties."

1&1 Internet Inc. offers telephone and online technical support, seven days per week, 24 hours per day. All of the online site design and management tools are easy to use, powerful, and allow people to establish their online businesses quickly and inexpensively. For someone using specialized software, such as Microsoft FrontPage to create her site, eShop is fully compatible with FrontPage extensions as well as other third-party software packages, such as Adobe DreamWeaver.

OSCommerce

> *Service provider*: OSCommerce
>
> *Website*: oscommerce.com
>
> *Turnkey solution pricing*: Free (Site Hosting Not Included)

If you're looking for extremely powerful and versatile e-commerce website development tools that will allow you to create the most professional and highly functional online business possible, look no further than OSCommerce. Unlike the "turnkey solutions" described in this chapter, OSCommerce is downloadable software that runs on your computer. It can be used to design, publish, and maintain an e-commerce website.

Although OSCommerce is not a complete turnkey solution in that it does not offer online hosting services for your online business, it does provide a free collection of development tools. Although this is extremely powerful software, it requires a learning curve and some basic programming knowledge to utilize fully. An alternative is to take advantage of the free OSCommerce website templates available for e-commerce and simply customize them.

The good news is that because OSCommerce is so popular, you'll have no trouble finding extremely talented programmers with the know-how to fully customize your e-commerce site using this software. All of the documentation you need to get started is provided, free of charge, from the OSCommerce website.

According to the software's creators, "OSCommerce is an online shop e-commerce solution that offers a wide range of out-of-the-box features that allow online stores to be set up fairly quickly with ease, and is available for free as an Open Source-based solution released under the GNU General Public License.

"OSCommerce was started in March 2000 and has since matured to a solution that is currently powering more than 13,000 registered live shops around the world. The success of OSCommerce is secured by a great and active community where members help one another out and participate in development issues reflecting upon the current state of the project. You are more than welcome to contribute to the success of OSCommerce by helping out in the realization of the project, by participating in the forums, by donating to the team developers and sponsoring the project, or just by spreading the word!"

For a listing of online stores currently operating OSCommerce, visit http://shops.oscommerce.com. The OSCommerce software is much more powerful and customizable than many of the turnkey solutions described in this chapter, but it's also more difficult to use, especially if you're not techo-savvy.

Pre-created OSCommerce templates are available from a wide range of sources. Some of these templates, which can be customized to meet your unique needs, are offered free of charge, while others are sold by their independent creators.

To find OSCommerce templates online, using any internet search engine, enter the search phrase "OSCommerce templates" or visit one of these ten sites:

1. algozone.com
2. myoscommercetemplates.com

CLICK TIP

When hiring a free-lance website designer or programmer, try to negotiate a flat-rate fee for a project, as opposed to an hourly fee. This will typically save you money and help ensure your project gets completed in a timely manner.

3. oscmax.com

4. oscommercecafe.com

5. oscommercetemplates.com

6. templatemonster.com/oscommerce-templates.php

7. templateworld.com/oscommerce.html

8. theoscommercestore.com

9. tornado-templates.com/oscommerce-templates .php

10. websitetemplatedesign.com

To have an e-commerce website created from scratch using the OSCommerce software or to have a template fully customized to meet the unique needs of your online business venture, you can find qualified programmers by using sites such as: eLance.com, getafreelancer.com, or Guru.com. Fees will vary greatly, so be sure to shop around and carefully evaluate a website designer's portfolio before hiring him.

Yahoo! Stores (Yahoo! Small Business Solutions)

Service provider: Yahoo!

Phone number: (866) 781-9246

Website: http://smallbusiness.yahoo.com/ecommerce/

Turnkey solution pricing: $39.95 to $299.95 per month (plus additional fees)

If you know anything about the internet or consider yourself an accomplished web surfer, you already know that Yahoo! is one of the most popular internet search engines and web directories. As a company, Yahoo! also offers a wide range of other services to internet users.

For online business operators, Yahoo! offers its Small Business Services division. It includes a robust e-commerce turnkey solution, called Yahoo! Stores as well as search engine marketing/advertising opportunities for promoting your online business (see Chapter 10).

No matter which of the Yahoo! Stores plans you purchase, you'll be given full access to the service's Store Design tools, which allow you to design a professional-looking site using a step-by-step wizard and templates that can be fully customized. Using this solution, you can sell up to 50,000 unique products and maintain your online business with the utmost ease.

Included with each Yahoo! Stores package is a fully secure shopping cart and checkout application that can also be fully customized. Although you can incorporate your own merchant account to accept credit card payments, Yahoo! Merchant Solutions has a partnership with Chase Paymentech and PayPal to offer fully compatible merchant account and online credit card processing options (for an additional fee).

The turnkey solution offered by Yahoo! also features a vast array of tools for marketing your business and driving traffic to your website, and a variety of order processing, inventory management, website traffic reporting, and book-keeping tools to make fulfilling orders and managing your customers easier and less time consuming.

Through Yahoo! Stores, Yahoo! Merchant Solutions truly offers a comprehensive e-commerce turnkey solution that's affordable, expandable, easy to use, and highly functional when it comes to designing, launching, and operating your online business venture. Best of all, you can get your online store up and running in hours using the service's Store Design tools.

As you grow and expand your website beyond the capabilities of the design tools offered, you'll discover that Yahoo! Stores is fully compatible with popular third-party applications, such as Adobe Dreamweaver, Adobe GoLive, and Microsoft Office FrontPage. Plus, telephone and online technical support is available 24 hours per day, seven days per week.

Yahoo! Stores has three different price plans, including the $39.95 per month Starter Plan. For additional functionality, the Standard Plan ($99.95 per month) is offered. It is ideal for online businesses generating between $12,000 and $80,000 per month. The Professional Plan, which is ideal for businesses generating more than $80,000 per month, is available for $299.95 per month. Depending on the plan you purchase and whether you prepay for service, discounts to the monthly fees are available.

In addition to the monthly fee, Yahoo! Merchant Solutions charges a per-transaction fee of between .75 percent and 1.5 percent of each transaction, depending on the Yahoo! Stores plan you sign up for. This added per-transaction fee is in addition to any credit card processing fees you may be responsible for.

According to Yahoo!, the transaction fee is "a fee to maintain the infrastructure that supports your e-commerce services and transaction processing. This fee is based on the final price of the product and is not calculated on shipping and taxes. For comparison, some large e-commerce companies spend roughly five to eight percent of their sales to maintain their e-commerce infrastructure. We charge just .75 to 1.5 percent for access to similar e-commerce infrastructure and services of a similar level of quality."

Because Yahoo! Merchant Solutions is so popular, you'll find many independent freelance programmers who can help you customize and design your website, incorporating functionality and features that go beyond what's offered using the supplied Store Design tools. For a listing of pre-approved programming professionals (additional fees will apply for their services), visit http://developernetwork.store.yahoo.com.

Currently thousands of online-based businesses operate using Yahoo! Stores. To see a sampling of these stores and what yours could look like, visit http://smallbusiness.yahoo.com/ecommerce/customerstores.php.

The tools and services offered by Yahoo! Small Business Services are among the most powerful and cost-effective in the industry. You'll find that Yahoo! Merchant Services is equipped to handle the needs of almost every type of online business venture, yet the tools are easy-to-use, even for non-techno-savvy people.

Growing Beyond Your Turnkey Solution

If you opt to use a complete e-commerce turnkey solution and your online-based business becomes successful, at some point your needs as well as the demands of your customers may grow beyond the capability of the online tools provided by your turnkey solution. When this happens, give yourself a pat on the back. You've officially become a successful and accomplished e-commerce entrepreneur who is operating a profitable online business venture.

To be able to grow and expand your website, it may become necessary to use third-party website creation and management tools, such as Adobe Dreamweaver. Using these programs, however, requires some basic programming knowledge, and there's a learning curve for proficiency with these applications. To make the transition seamless, you'll probably want to hire freelance programmers and/or website designers who can handle much of the technical stuff for you. To learn more about some of the popular third-party website development tools available, visit these websites:

➡ Adobe Creative Suite 3—adobe.com/products/creativesuite
➡ Adobe Dreamweaver CS3—adobe.com/products/dreamweaver

➡ Adobe Flash—adobe.com/products/flash
➡ Adobe Photoshop CS3—adobe.com/products/photoshop/family
➡ eCommerce—oscommerce.com
➡ LaGarde—storefront.net
➡ Lite Commerce—litecommerce.com
➡ Merchandizer—merchandizer.com
➡ Microsoft Office FrontPage—http://office.microsoft.com/en-us/front page/default.aspx
➡ Microsoft SharePoint Designer 2007—http://office.microsoft.com/en-us/ sharepointdesigner

Understanding E-Commerce Website Design Fundamentals

As important as it is to have a great idea for a product (or products) to sell online, it's equally important to develop a site that appeals to your target audience and transforms visitors to your site into paying customers who place their orders online for your products.

What's Next

Once you've selected a complete e-commerce turnkey solution that you believe is best suited to the needs of your business venture, you need to begin designing the look of your website and creating its content. The next chapter will introduce you to important design fundamentals and provide valuable tips for creating a website that looks professional, is easy to navigate, is welcoming to your customers, and provides the functionality needed for your business to become successful.

Chapter 7

Website Design Fundamentals

*D*esigning the layout and look of your e-commerce website and selecting appropriate content for it is critical. Your goal throughout the design process must be to create a site that is visually pleasing, extremely easy to navigate, and highly informative. Each and every element of your site—the text, graphics, animations, photographs, video, and audio—must work together seamlessly to sell your product, convey your marketing message, enhance your company's image and credibility, and make it easy for your customers to place their orders with the utmost of confidence.

Before you can start designing your website, you must already know:

➡ the target audience of your website;
➡ the product you'll be selling;
➡ your primary marketing message; and
➡ the assets you have available to incorporate into the site.

Next, you need to determine what information and specific content you plan on incorporating into your site, and how that information will be distributed throughout the various pages. If you surf other e-commerce sites, you'll find that virtually all share common elements. The most successful sites offer a very simple and straightforward layout. All of the information a potential customer could want or need is easy to find and readily available with a few clicks of the mouse.

A well-designed website is comprised of a handful of individual web pages. Ultimately, aside from your site's homepage and shopping cart, what other pages you incorporate into your site is entirely up to you. The next section focuses on some of the common content you could add to your site.

The word that should be in the forefront of your thoughts as you design your site is "continuity." From an overall design, layout, and visual standpoint, each page should fit nicely with the others and maintain a consistent look, attitude, and tone. Thus, you'll probably want to use the same fonts, type styles, and color scheme, for example.

Individual Web Pages that Comprise a Quality E-Commerce Website

Savvy web surfers spend a lot of time visiting different websites. They know that from a website's main page, they can often find information about the company by clicking on a Company Information, About Us, or Company Background icon or menu option. Likewise, as they're reading a product description for something they'd like to order, they already know to click on the Add to Cart or Buy Now icon to add that item to their shopping cart and begin the ordering process.

It All Starts from Your Site's Homepage

When a web surfer types your company's URL into his browser or clicks on a link to your website, your homepage is where they'll wind up. The content of your homepage is the first thing a potential customer sees, so it's essential that you make a positive first impression extremely quickly.

The look, layout, overall design, and content of your homepage sets the tone for your entire site. Thus, it should be welcoming and informative, and get the potential customer excited about learning more about what you have to offer. Because web surfers have a very short attention span, they'll leave and probably won't ever return if they don't find exactly what they're looking for within the first five to ten seconds or if they don't feel comfortable visiting your site.

The website template you use to design your site will help you establish a professional looking layout. However, ultimately you must determine what content and information will be incorporated into your site. These are decisions that are based on what you're selling, what message you're attempting to communicate, who your target audience is, and your own personal preferences.

Your homepage should incorporate the following core elements (listed in alphabetical order):

➡ *Company logo.* This graphic should be displayed prominently at the top of your homepage, as well as on every other page of your site. A logo is a unique visual graphic, which can, but does not have to, display the company's name. It uniquely identifies your company. Logos are used to help create brand or product awareness.

➡ *Company name.* In text form, as well as through the use of a graphic logo, your company's name should appear prominently at the top of your homepage and on all subsequent pages within your site.

➡ *Contact information.* Every page of your website should display your company's phone number (preferably toll-free) as well as your e-mail address so customers know they can reach you with their questions or place their order by telephone if they're not comfortable completing an online order form. Making a phone number available to your customers enhances your company's credibility and your customer's confidence in you. On your website's Contact Us page, you can display your full mailing address and multiple e-mail addresses for various people or divisions within your organization.

➡ *Copyright and privacy policy information.* At the very bottom of your homepage, in small type, include a copyright notice, trademark information, and a link to your company's privacy policy (if applicable).

➡ *Navigation bar/menu.* From your site's navigation bar or main menu, the visitor should be able to access all of the important web pages that comprise your site.

➡ *Product categories.* When displayed as a menu or collection of links, a user can search for products based on a category. For example, if you're selling men's clothing, categories might include: casual shirts, dress shirts, pants, suits, shoes, underwear, and sleepwear. If you'll be offering a collection of products, dividing them into categories and being able to display similar products within a category make it easier for customers to review all of your offerings of interest.

➡ *Search box.* When this feature is incorporated into a site, it allows visitors to find exactly what they're looking for by entering a keyword, search phrase, or product number. It can be a powerful navigational tool to help people quickly find exactly what they're looking for.

➡ *Specials or promotions box.* This is the place on your homepage to promote your daily or weekly specials. Are you offering a buy-one, get-one-free offer? Perhaps free shipping on orders over $100, or a 10 percent off discount if someone places her order by a specific date. Use this portion of your homepage to generate urgency and build further interest in your products.

➡ *Store/company description.* While the About Us or Company Information page of your site should contain a detailed description of your company, its management, and its history, adding a short, well-written description of your company on your homepage provides an immediate introduction for your customers and offers a preview of what they can expect from the site. Keep this down to one or two sentences.

Your homepage serves as the main hub for the rest of your site. From here, a visitor should be able to quickly access any content on your site with just one or two clicks of the mouse. From this page, people (whether they're web savvy or not) should be able to find product information, learn about your company, discover your company's policies, make contact with you directly, and quickly link to your site's shopping cart so they can place their order with ease.

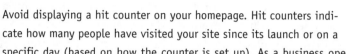

WARNING

Avoid displaying a hit counter on your homepage. Hit counters indicate how many people have visited your site since its launch or on a specific day (based on how the counter is set up). As a business operator, knowing this information is essential, but it's not something you want to advertise to your competition or customers. If someone visits your site at 3 P.M. and the displayed counter is at 31,503, for example, and two days later they revisit your site and the counter is only at 31,510, this indicates very few people have visited your site. It could plant a seed of doubt in a potential customer's mind about your company's popularity and credibility.

Other Individual Web Pages to Incorporate within Your Site

While every e-commerce website will be different, most online business owners find the need to incorporate the following pages or content into their site in order to provide a comprehensive marketing and sales solution for their product. Based on what you're selling, your target audience, and your online sales approach, not all of these pages or types of content may be relevant to your venture.

The following (listed in alphabetical order) are the most common individual web pages that should be incorporated into your e-commerce site and the type of content that should be incorporated into it:

➡ *Blog, podcast, or newsletter.* One way to enhance customer loyalty, teach people more about your products, increase repeat orders, and build brand awareness is to offer a regularly published (daily, weekly, or monthly) blog, podcast, or downloadable newsletter. You'll want to communicate your marketing message within your blog, podcast, or newsletter, but they should also include information that is seen as informative and valuable to your customers: how-to articles or tips for saving time or money when using your product. Use your creativity to provide news and information that your customers will be interested in. While you can offer this as a free download from your website, you can also have an opt-in e-mail list that people subscribe to in order to have your blog, podcast, or newsletter sent directly to their inbox.

➡ *Company Information, About Us, or Company Background.* Use this page to tell your company's story, describe its philosophies, explain why your company and its products are different from your competition, and illustrate how your products are unique or special. You can also include short biographies of your company's executives, which helps to build credibility. Keep your company information down to one page or one screen's worth of information.

➡ *Contact Us.* One of the most powerful ways you can quickly build potential customers' confidence in your business is to make yourself available to answer their questions, address their concerns, and handle their problems. In addition to displaying a toll-free telephone number, be sure to display your company's full mailing address and e-mail address. If you have a customer service department, returns department, public relations/marketing department, advertising department, etc., list contact information for each division separately. Making your customers feel that they can reach you easily if they experience problems or have questions allows them to feel more confident in placing an order.

➡ *Customer testimonials.* Offering a page that reproduces customer testimonials relating to your company and its products is a great way to increase a potential customer's confidence and enhance your company's credibility. Keep the testimonials short and to the point, but make sure they're positive, believable, accurate, truthful, and informative.

➡ *FAQ.* No matter how straightforward and easy to understand the information about your products and your company's policies are, visitors to your website will still have questions about pricing, product specifications, how to place an order, return policies, etc. FAQ (frequently asked questions) documents usually adhere to a question-and-answer format and are used to answer the most common questions potential customers have. Use well-written text. Making this information available on your site reduces the amount of direct contact (via phone or e-mail) you have with customers. These documents also allow you to communicate important information in an easy-to-understand format. You can create separate FAQ documents that describe: how to use your product, the top features of your product, how to place an order, your company's return policies, or answers to the most common questions your customers have.

➡ *News, sales, and promotions.* This page of your website can be used just like a weekly circular or print advertisement to promote news about your company and its products, and sales or promotions.

➡ *Online ordering/shopping cart.* When visitors are ready to place an order for your products, they click on a Buy Now or Order icon, for example, and get linked to your site's shopping cart. The shopping cart is an online order form that allows your customers to input their order-related information (including their payment details) and have the order processed (often in real time). The turnkey e-commerce website solution you use will include a shopping cart, but it's essential that the shopping cart application built into your site be easy to use and include all of the functionality that's necessary for your customers to quickly place their order online.

➡ *Press room.* Part of your business's success strategy should be to utilize a public relations campaign to generate publicity about your business and its products (see Chapter 9). The Press Room area of your website should contain an online press kit, copies of press releases, high-resolution product photography, and contact information for members of the media (reporters, journalists, and editors) to reach you quickly. When members of the media are working on stories, they're typically under very tight deadlines. If you make all of the information they need available on your site, your chances of receiving free publicity and having your products mentioned in articles, features, or news stories increase dramatically. The Press Room area of your website can also be used to showcase publicity your company or its products have already received.

CLICK TIP

To help improve your search engine optimization efforts (see Chapter 10), product descriptions should appear within your website as text whenever possible, not as part of graphic elements. Doing so allows search engine spiders or crawlers to easily find, categorize, and catalog your site's content appropriately, which in turn helps boost your search engine placement and ranking on most popular search engines.

➡ *Product description/catalog pages.* For an e-commerce website, your product description and/or catalog pages are absolutely critical. It's here your customers learn about what products you're offering through detailed, well-written descriptions and by viewing product photography. Although you want to keep your product descriptions relatively short, they must also be comprehensive, informative, accurate, and easy to understand, and contain all the details customers will want to know before they place their order. All of your product descriptions should be consistent in format and tone, and should be targeted specifically to your primary audience. You want to include a Buy, Order, or Add to Cart icon with each product description so people can quickly order the product online. You might also opt to include customer reviews of your products.

➡ *Return Policy/Guarantee/Warrantee.* Displaying this information for your customers will boost their confidence before they place their order. An important aspect of good customer service is explaining up front how your company handles problems and a customer's need or desire to return products. If you charge a restocking fee for returns or issue refunds within 15 days, these policies should be spelled out on your site. Keep in mind that your customers will appreciate a 30-day, no-questions-asked, unconditional return policy that has no restocking fee. The easier it is for customers to handle returns, the more confident they'll be in taking a chance on buying products, sight unseen, from your website. If your product comes with a guarantee or warrantee, this should also be well promoted to boost customer confidence.

➡ *Splash page.* Some websites use fancy opening animation to introduce people to their website. This is called a *splash page*, because it's supposed to make a splash when people see it. The goal of a splash page is to generate a "wow" effect. The problem with splash pages is that they look great, but take valuable time to load and typically say absolutely nothing about the company or its products. In other words, for most e-commerce websites, they're an utter waste of time. If potential customers have to wait even five seconds for a site's splash page to load, you run a high risk of losing them before they've even visited your site. Remember, your potential customers are visiting your site to learn about and/or buy a product, not be entertained by a fancy graphic animation sequence before they're permitted to visit your site's real homepage.

➡ *Technical Support/Customer Service.* Depending on what you're selling, it may be necessary or appropriate to offer ongoing technical support to existing customers via telephone, online through live chats, or e-mail, for example. Having an area of your website dedicated to helping customers use your products once they order them improves customer loyalty and helps generate repeat orders. It also increases your chances of receiving positive word-of-mouth advertising. One of your ongoing goals in terms of your business operations should be to provide the most professional, helpful, friendly, and accessible customer service possible. In some cases, customers will go out of their way or pay more for products if they know they'll be supported by top-notch customer service or technical support from the company they make the purchase from.

Top Ten Website Design Tips

This section contains ten site design tips you'll definitely want to consider throughout the design process. The feedback you receive from your testers (see the next section of this chapter) should help you better target these tips toward your target customers.

Tip 1: Keep the Site's Design Visually Simple

The fonts, type styles, text colors, background colors, photographs, and other graphic elements you incorporate into your site contribute to its overall appearance. Your goal is to create a professional and appealing look for your site by customizing the template you're working with. Putting too much information on a page, using text that's too small or difficult to read, or utilizing a color scheme that's not visually appealing detract from the experience your visitors have. If you look at some of the most successful e-commerce sites such as Amazon.com, Target.com, or Apple.com, you'll notice their layout is extremely simple, inviting, and visually appealing. While you never want to copy another site exactly, you can take design ideas from other sites and incorporate them into your own with proper customization.

Tip 2: Make Sure Your Site Is Easy to Navigate

If you confuse your potential customers, you lose them. With a click of their mouse, they'll be off surfing to another site, probably your competitor's. No matter where on your site visitors happen to be, it should be obvious to them where they should go next or how they can quickly return to where they just were. If they're looking for something specific on your site, such as your product's technical specifications or your company's return policy, they should be able to find that information intuitively and quickly.

Tip 3: Avoid Using Excessive Bells and Whistles

Just because you *can* add animations, video footage, sound effects, and other eye-catching effects to your site, that doesn't mean they're necessary or beneficial. Focus on the very best way to communicate your particular sales message and educate people about your product using the simplest and quickest methods possible. Don't use three paragraphs of text, for example, if the same information can be conveyed in a single photograph.

If you're going to use special effects, make sure this added content won't distract visitors, waste their time (while they're waiting for a useless animation to load), or confuse them. Effects are great for entertainment-oriented websites or games, but when people are trying to learn about a product or make a purchase, they want the process to happen efficiently.

Tip 4: Use Professional-Quality Product Photos and Artwork

Because visitors to your site can't touch and feel your products as they could in a traditional retail store, they'll rely on your product photographs to learn about the product. The photographs you use must be crystal clear, enlargeable (with a click of the mouse), detailed, and offer an accurate depiction of what you're selling. For this reason, seriously consider using custom photographs created by a professional photographer or pictures from the manufacturer of your products (if you can obtain permission to use this artwork).

Over time, you might want to learn how to take quality photographs, but as you're attempting to launch your online business, you have more important uses for your time. For a few hundred dollars, hire a professional photographer to provide you with the quality photos of your product you need.

By showcasing blurry photos, photos taken in poor lighting conditions, or photos that don't properly show off your product, you'll be taking away from your product's appeal. Your customers rely on your product photos to help them make their decision to buy.

If the background in the product photos is too busy or its color clashes with the rest of your site's design elements, it will also take away from the professional look of your site. So, it's usually a good idea to use a solid white background, solid black background, or have no background in your product shots. Whatever your choice, make sure you're consistent in all product photos on your site.

To complement your custom product photography, you can use images on your website that you license and acquire from a stock photo agency. Agencies can supply professional images depicting almost anything.

Tip 5: Make It Very Easy for People to Contact You

A great thing about cyberspace is that you can operate your e-commerce site from anywhere and potentially attract shoppers from all over the world. For some people, buying a product sight unseen from a company they can't physically visit is extremely intimidating. And, many people are concerned about credit card fraud and identity theft that might result from shopping with credit cards online.

In addition to creating a professional-looking and informative site that boosts confidence, one of the easiest ways to eliminate many of the fears people have about online shopping is to offer them an opportunity to make direct contact with you by telephone, e-mail, online chat, or U.S. mail. If someone can

CLICK TIP

When a (potential) customer does make contact with you, it is essential to provide top-notch customer service that's professional, helpful, efficient, and friendly.

pick up the phone, dial a toll-free number, and quickly get questions answered or concerns addressed, she'll be must more willing to shop from your site and become a customer.

Tip 6: Be Honest

Everything on your site should be focused on communicating the absolute truth to your customers. If your product descriptions, product photographs, company background information, or any other content on your site doesn't come across as being upfront and honest, you'll lose credibility and your visitors will simply shop elsewhere. Sure, it's OK to use colorful language to advertise and market your product. However, never over embellish the truth, make false statements, make promises you can't keep, or intentionally mislead your potential customers.

If someone receives the product they've ordered from your company and it doesn't live up to the expectations you helped create based on information on your website, it will be returned. When this happens, not only will you have lost a customer, but chances are, they'll tell other people about their negative experience dealing with you.

Tip 7: Convey the Information You Know Potential Customers Want and Need

The easiest way to convey information is to put yourself in your customers' shoes and think carefully about their wants and needs. Chapter 2 offers information about getting to know your target customers. As you create the content for your website, focus on communicating your information quickly and efficiently, knowing the attention span of your visitors is short.

Tip 8: Eliminate All Errors and Typos

It's essential that you carefully and repeatedly proofread the content on your site. It should contain absolutely no typos or errors. Depending on the amount of text on your site, for example, you might opt to hire a professional editor to proofread the content of your site before it goes live. At the very least, have several people (in addition to yourself) proofread everything carefully.

In addition to fixing typographical or grammatical errors in your text, make sure all of the photo captions describe the appropriate photos, all of the graphics are placed correctly, and all of the links on your page lead to the correct destinations. Web surfers find it extremely frustrating to click on a dead link or one that leads to the wrong place. Even the smallest errors on your site detract from the professional image you're trying to establish.

Tip 9: Ensure the Site Is Compatible with All Commonly Used Web Browsers

There are only a handful of commonly used web browsers out there: Microsoft Explorer, Mozilla's FireFox, and Apple's Safari. And although Netscape Navigator is no longer formally supported, plenty of web surfers still use it as their primary browser.

Each of these browsers is slightly different, so it's important to take basic compatibility issues into consideration when designing your website or customizing a template. Before opening for business, test your site using each popular web browser, and be sure to fix any formatting or compatibility issues.

The AnyBrowser.com website (anybrowser.com) offers a collection of free tools and online resources designed for site publishers to help make their site compatible with all popular browsers. Keynote's Net Mechanic (netmechanic.com/products/Browser-Tutorial.shtml) also offers tools for making a site compatible with all popular web browsers and offers tutorials for overcoming incompatibility issues between browsers.

WARNING

Even if your website looks perfect on the latest version of Microsoft's Internet Explorer, for example, it might not be compatible with an older (but still commonly used) version of this browser, not to mention other popular browsers. If your site is not compatible with a browser, that impacts how it appears when someone visits your site. Formatting, fonts, and colors may be altered, and some functionality may be impeded. Even if you're using a template for your site's design, make sure it's fully compatible with all popular browsers for both PC and Mac computers, or you could alienate potential customers and make it difficult or impossible for them to visit and shop from your site.

Tip 10: Start with Enough Investment Capital

If you're a first-time online business owner, start off small by offering one or just a few products initially, and focus on selling those products to your target audience. As your business becomes successful, you can branch out by offering more products or product variations, and begin targeting a larger customer base.

Every online business has a learning curve associated with getting it up and running. It also takes time for your business to be profitable. As you develop your business plan and preliminary budget, determine how much money it'll take to launch your business and keep it running for several months (potentially 6 to 12 months) without generating a profit. How quickly your business becomes profitable depends on a wide range of factors, including the profit margin associated with the products you're selling.

In addition to establishing a realistic startup and operating budget, be sure to plan for the unexpected. There will be added costs and fees along the way that didn't get included in your first budget but will need to be covered to successfully launch and operate your business. Having enough money on hand to cover all the costs associated with running your business until it becomes profitable could mean the difference between ultimate success and failure. If you have to start cutting corners and taking short cuts to keep your business going or just to get it launched, your chances of encountering obstacles and problems increase exponentially.

Know Your Customer's Surfing Capabilities

Not all web surfers access the internet using a high-speed DSL, Broadband, or FIOS connection. In fact, according to Leichtman Research Group, in 2007, out of the 53 percent of American homes that had access to the internet, around 47 percent (about 33 million U.S. users) still use a slow, dial-up connection.

According to its report, "Broadband adoption is affected by household income. Broadband reaches 68 percent of households with annual income over $50,000. By contrast, 39 percent of households with income under $50,000 subscribe to broadband services."

Thanks to improving technologies, lower prices, and the growing popularity of the internet, Jupiter Research reports that adoption of high-speed internet services is expected to reach 70 percent of all U.S. households by 2012.

Make sure your site (or a version of your site) works well for people using a slow internet connection. Also, avoid incorporating features into your site that require browser plug-ins that aren't common. Although many web surfers have added a Flash player and/or PDF file reader plug-in to their

CLICK TIP

Depending on your target audience, you might also consider creating a version of your site that's compatible (and easily readable) using a wireless PDA, Smartphone, or cell phone web browser. The Apple iPhone is just one example of a cell phone with a full-featured web browser, but it currently lacks the ability to display Flash animations, which are often part of websites. As an e-commerce business operator, your site (or a version of it) must cater to the limitations of cell phone and wireless PDA web browsers if you wish to target them.

browser, there are plenty of plug-ins that are far less popular. If your site requires the use of a less popular plug-in, you will greatly reduce the number of web surfers capable of visiting and ordering from your site. Focus on catering to the broadest audience of web surfers possible, unless you know that the majority of people in your target audience is web savvy and utilize a high-speed connection.

Seek Out Website Testers Before Launching Your Site

As an online entrepreneur, you're probably too close to the project emotionally to maintain a proper perspective when it comes to determining if your site's content truly appeals to its target audience and has achieved its objective. One way to ensure you achieve your objective of creating the most welcoming, informative, and easy-to-navigate site possible is to invite friends, coworkers, potential customers, and people you know to explore your site before it's officially published and launched. Solicit detailed feedback from your testers by having them answer the 25 questions in Figure 7.1: Website Evaluation Worksheet. Their answers will help you improve your website before it actually launches.

The people you ask to test your site should not necessarily be familiar

CLICK TIP

For the people who serve as your site testers, consider offering them either free product as a thank-you, or provide them with a significant discount on their first order from your site.

> *Figure 7.1:* **WEBSITE EVALUATION WORKSHEET**
>
> 1. Is the website visually appealing?
>
> 2. Is the website easy to understand?
>
> 3. Were you able to find product information quickly and easily?
>
> 4. Were you able to find and use the shopping cart without confusion?
>
> 5. Would you order from this company with confidence?
>
> 6. What would you incorporate into the site to make it more welcoming, informative, or easier to use?
>
> 7. How would you compare this site with its competition, and other sites you've visited in the past?
>
> 8. Based on what you've learned from this site, what would you say is the most important or useful information about its products?
>
> 9. Did you find any errors or typos on the site? If so, where?
>
> 10. Do the product photos featured on the site reveal enough detail about what it's selling?
>
> 11. Based on your experience surfing other sites, what elements or features is this site lacking?
>
> 12. Did the site builder incorporate too much, too little, or just the right amount of information and content on each individual web page within the site?
>
> 13. Did you find the homepage welcoming and informative?
>
> 14. Do you believe the company's policies, guarantee, and warranty are fair and easy to understand?
>
> 15. Did you feel confident in your ability to reach the customer service department via telephone, e-mail, or online chat in order to get your questions answered or your concerns addressed?
>
> 16. At any point did you get lost or confused while navigating around the website? If so, where and why?

Figure 7.1: **WEBSITE EVALUATION WORKSHEET,** continued

17. Are the product descriptions accurate and detailed enough?

18. Did you find any of the product descriptions misleading in anyway?

19. From a readability standpoint, is all of the text on the site easy to read? Is the text too small, too large, or too cluttered? Are the fonts, type styles, text colors, and/or background colors visually appealing or distracting?

20. In your option, what are the best and worst features of the website overall?

21. Are the prices competitive?

22. After visiting the site for the first time, would you be likely to place an order right away, or would you first shop around and compare the site to its competitors?

23. What is one feature or piece of content on the website that you would change to make it better? How would you improve it?

24. Is there any information about the company or products that you could not easily and quickly find on the site? If so, what?

25. What would prevent you from placing an order on the website during your first visit?

with your products, but they should be people you perceive to be your potential customers. They should not have a technical background. In other words, find people who are not programmers or professional website designers. You want everyday web surfers to explore your site and offer their honest feedback.

What's Next

Every online business must be able to accept online payments. It's this ability to sell products on the internet directly from your site that separates an e-commerce website from a marketing-oriented site that simply conveys product information.

CLICK TIP

Check out what works for other websites. Thanks to statistics and information that's published about other e-commerce websites, you can easily determine what works well and what doesn't simply by visiting and learning from the most successful e-commerce websites. Obviously, you'd also want to avoid the mistakes made by the least successful sites. *Internet Retailer* magazine publishes a list of the top 500 retail websites each year. It can be found at internet retailer.com/top500/list.asp.

The next chapter focuses on some of the popular online payment options you can add to your site in order to streamline the order-taking process and offer your customers choices about how they'd like to pay for their purchases.

While your business will benefit from having its own credit card merchant account, you can also offer online payment options, such as Google Checkout and PayPal Express Checkout, which are described in greater detail in the next chapter.

Chapter 8

Alternative Online Payment Options

*T*he primary difference between an ordinary website and an e-commerce site is that the latter accepts online orders and is designed to be an online business, not just a marketing or promotional tool or a vehicle for disseminating information.

When someone places an order on your site using the online payment services made available, she can complete her purchase and initiate payment using one of the following options:

➡ Submit her credit card, debit card, or electronic check information online (assuming the seller has a merchant account and is able to accept Visa, MasterCard, American Express, and/or Discover)
➡ Call your company's (toll-free) phone number and place her order via telephone
➡ Mail in a personal or company check
➡ Ask to have her order shipped COD or charged against her credit line with your company (via purchase order)
➡ Wire money between the buyer's and seller's bank accounts

Two other online payment options that are quickly becoming popular among online shoppers and merchants alike are Google Checkout and PayPal Express Checkout. This chapter focuses on these two services and discusses why you might want to offer them as payment options to your customers.

As an online merchant, the ability to accept major credit cards is essential to the success of your business. Your customers want the convenience and security associated with making their purchases using their credit card, just as they would if they shopped at traditional retail stores. By also accepting debit cards and electronic checks, you're opening up your potential customer base to consumers who don't necessarily have a major credit card.

The other payment alternatives give your customers additional options. However, giving them too many options can easily create confusion. Your goal as an online merchant is to create a shopping experience that's quick, convenient, secure, and straightforward. The fewer mouse clicks and data entry someone has to do to complete an order, the better.

During the design phase of your site, pinpoint the information you need to collect from your customers during the order-taking process. Next, determine the quickest and most efficient way to collect that information. It will probably include the following:

➡ The purchaser's name
➡ Billing address
➡ Recipient's name
➡ Shipping address
➡ Customer's telephone number
➡ Customer's e-mail address
➡ The name on the buyer's credit card

CLICK TIP

Ideally, you'll want to provide your customers with the option of having their basic information saved so when they return to your site to place future orders, they don't need to re-enter all their personal information. From a merchant's standpoint, this functionality is added using cookies, a concept that is familiar to all website designers. It may or may not be offered as part of your e-commerce turnkey solution.

➡ The actual credit card number, expiration date, and its three-digit security code

➡ Details about the item the customer wishes to order (quantity, item name, item number, size, color, etc.).

The Benefits of Google Checkout and PayPal Express Checkout

To make shopping online a more secure, faster experience to all consumers who opt to participate, both Google Checkout and PayPal Express Checkout have developed services that allow customers to create a single password-protected account (with either Google or PayPal) and enter all their personal and financial information just once.

CLICK TIP

If it takes customers too-long to make their purchase on your website, or the check-out process is too confusing, they quickly become frustrated and shop elsewhere. Your goal is to transform as many visitors to your site into paying customers as is possible. When calculated as a percentage, the number of visitors to your site who make a purchase (vs. leave without making a purchase) is referred to as your "conversion rate." When a consumer visits your site, starts the buying process, but ultimate decides against making the purchase, that's referred to as "cart abandonment." Offering an express checkout process through Google Checkout or PayPal Express Checkout reduces cart abandonment for many online merchants.

When a participating consumer opts to make an online purchase with any participating online merchant, the customer needs only to click on the Google Checkout or PayPal icon that's incorporated into a site's shopping cart. The consumer is then seamlessly transferred to either the Google or PayPal system, which already has their name, address, and credit card data stored. This eliminates the need for the consumer to repeatedly enter this information whenever they place an order with a particular online merchant.

A consumer can feel safer using Google Checkout, for example, because the merchant they're shopping with never actually receives their personal credit card information. Instead, Google processes the payment (and then pays the merchant). The consumer also doesn't need to remember usernames and passwords for every online merchant he shops with. At any time he can review his purchase history, track orders and deliveries, or contact merchants he's done business with—all from one centralized website operated by Google or PayPal.

For consumers, Google Checkout or PayPal is totally free. They can set up their own secure account in minutes and there is no extra charge associated with making purchases using either system. The merchant, however, pays fees to use these services.

Theoretically, an online merchant can accept major credit card, debit card, and electronic check payments using either services and not have a separate merchant account. However, if a customer has not set up a Google Checkout or PayPal account (and does not wish to do so), she could not place an online order on your site.

The number of consumers who have either a Google Checkout or PayPal account is growing quickly, but as of early 2008, is not yet at the point where an online merchant could only accept these payment options and not have her own merchant account. Currently, offering either or both of these online payment options should be considered an added convenience merchants extend to their customers.

As of early 2008, PayPal boasted a network of 150 million active accounts that continues to grow at a rate of 104,500 new accounts opened every day. Google Checkout is a newer service but is being actively marketed to both consumers and merchants in hopes of making it an accepted standard for online payments.

PayPal accepts foreign currencies, so you can immediately begin tapping the worldwide market with your online business. In fact, PayPal reports it accepts payments in 16 currencies and allows merchants to sell to shoppers in 190 countries and regions. For the consumer, their Google Checkout or PayPal account can store an unlimited number of shipping addresses and credit cards.

Google Checkout

Launched in June 2006, Google Checkout is much newer than PayPal, but it carries the Google brand name and is quickly becoming a popular way for consumers to pay for their online purchases. One of the many ways Google is attracting customers to a free Google Checkout account is to offer an ongoing array of money-saving offers and promotions when the service is used. For example, during the 2007 holiday season, customers earned two frequent flier miles (on the airline of their choice) per dollar spent using Google Checkout. Other holiday promotions included free shipping from participating merchants and an instant savings of $10 to $50 off of their online order.

For merchants, one benefit of Google Checkout is that they can utilize the Google Checkout logo or shopping cart logo in their online advertising, including within Google AdWords ads. These logos instantly identify your online business as supporting Google Checkout, so your potential customers know they can expect a quick, secure, and easy online shopping experience. Thousands of well-known merchants, and plenty of startups, currently support Google Checkout. For a partial listing of merchants, visit google.com/checkout/m.html.

CLICK TIP

Fred Lerner from Ritz Interactive (ritzinteractive.com) reports, "The new Google Checkout badge that appears on our AdWords advertisements has given us a 23 percent lift in clickthrough rate. And customers that use Google Checkout convert 24 percent more frequently than those that go through our standard checkout process." Brandon Hartness, from Golfballs.com added, "Conversion rates for shoppers using Google Checkout are about 40 percent higher than shoppers using other forms of checkout and payment."

Unlike PayPal, Google Checkout is a checkout flow, not a form of payment or a person-to-person money transfer service. When people make a payment using Google Checkout, they're ultimately paying with the major credit card that's on file with the service. According to Google, "The goal of Google Checkout is to help you offer your buyers a fast, safe, and convenient buying experience, not to replace any existing payment types your buyers use."

Currently, Google Checkout is designed to be used by online merchants for transactions involving tangible and digital goods (including downloadable products). However, payments can also be processed for services or subscriptions as long as all transactions adhere to Goggle's stated content policies.

As of February 1, 2008, the fees to merchants using Google Checkout were 2 percent of each sale, plus a $.20 per-transaction fee. There are no monthly fees, set-up charges, or gateway service fees. Depending on the deal you have with your merchant account provider, these rates are extremely competitive. One potential drawback is that Google Checkout only accepts U.S. funds, so it won't work for processing international sales.

If you are an online merchant using Google AdWords as part of your advertising and marketing efforts (see Chapter 10), you may be eligible for free transaction processing. As of early 2008, for every $1 spent on AdWords each month, a merchant could process $10 in sales the following month for free through Google Checkout.

There are a few other potential fees and charges an online merchant should be aware of. For example, if a consumer initiates a chargeback, the merchant will be responsible for a $10 chargeback fee.

As an online merchant, once you register to accept Google Checkout payments, you'll be able to add a Google Checkout icon to your shopping cart. This icon is available in three sizes (180 x 46 pixels, 168 x 44 pixels and 160 x 43 pixels). It should be placed next to every existing checkout button currently on your site. (The checkout button typically appears on your Shopping Cart page.)

CLICK TIP

Google maintains an official Google Checkout Blog for merchants. It can be accessed, free of charge, by visiting http://googlecheckout.blogspot.com. Here, you'll find a vast quantity of information about how merchants can best utilize this service to improve sales and profits.

For online merchants using a shopping cart application offered by one of the dozens of third-party companies, integrating Google Checkout on your site takes just minutes. For a current list of compatible shopping cart applications, visit http://checkout.google.com/seller/integrate_getnew.html. If your site has been custom created, Google offers the necessary tools (free) to quickly integrate Google Checkout. Visit http://checkout.google.com/seller/developers.html for details.

PayPal Express Checkout

According to PayPal, in early 2008, "Account holders transact an average of over $8.1 billion USD through PayPal every quarter. That's $2 million USD per hour, and over $48 million USD per day. Plus, over $750 million USD is stored in PayPal accounts, which is turned over every two weeks. Stored balances encourage impulse purchases and increased buying . . . . Over 80 percent of users say they're more likely to buy from an online business a second time if that business accepts PayPal . . . . With the PayPal Express Checkout button on your site, you can increase sales by 14 percent on average. Express Checkout conversion is 40 percent higher than other checkouts."

Unlike Google Checkout, PayPal allows online shoppers to set up a free account and make online payments via a major credit card, debit card, or electronic check. It's also possible for someone to maintain a balance in a PayPal account and make purchases using funds from that account.

Like Google Checkout, online merchants can easily incorporate a PayPal Express Checkout feature on the shopping cart page of their site. Using this feature, customers do not need to re-enter their address and credit card information in conjunction with each purchase.

When one of your customers completes the shopping cart on your site (indicating what he'd like to order), he'd click on the PayPal Express Check Out icon, instead of your site's regular Check Out icon. Now, he'll be instantly forwarded to the PayPal site, where he simply enters his username and password, selects a ship-to address and billing address, and processes his payment with a click of the mouse. He'll return to your site for confirmation of the order. The process takes just seconds, and as the merchant, you immediately receive the funds in your own PayPal account (which can be linked to your bank account).

For merchants, PayPal makes it easy to create their own customized shopping cart that's compatible with Express Check Out. You can also easily incorporate Buy Now, Add to Cart, View Cart, Donate, or Subscribe buttons within your site.

To begin accepting PayPal payments, as a merchant you need to set up either a Business or Premier account with PayPal. (Visit the paypal.com website and click on the "Selling with PayPal" link.) Currently, more than 100,000 e-commerce websites accept PayPal payments, including BN.com, eBay.com, Overstock.com, 1800flowers.com, U.S. Airways, iTunes.com, and Monster.com.

If you're creating your website from scratch and have signed with PayPal as a merchant, you can select a third-party shopping cart for your site that has PayPal pre-integrated (using website payments standard) or use the directions provided for incorporating PayPal into your own shopping cart application. For information about PayPal's compatibility with the various e-commerce turnkey solutions, call PayPal Integration Support at (888) 221-1161.

As a merchant, signing up for a PayPal account takes just minutes. Processing your bank account information, however, takes three to five business days. Using PayPal Website Payments Pro (paypal.com/pro) allows you to accept credit cards directly on your website, even if the customer does not have a PayPal account. This plan offers the same functionality as having a traditional credit card merchant account. For this service, you pay an ongoing $30 per month fee plus a 2.2 to 2.9 percent fee per order, in addition to a $.30 per-transaction fee. (The $.30 fee applies to each credit card authorization attempt.)

The Website Payments Standard plan from PayPal has no monthly fee, a 1.9 to 2.9 percent fee per sale, plus a $.30 per transaction fee. This plan requires customers to be transferred to the PayPal site and have a PayPal

CLICK TIP

E-commerce sites set up using a turn-key solution, such as Yahoo! Stores, eBay ProStores, or GoDaddy.com's Quick Shopping Cart (see Chapter 8) have built-in PayPal integration, so adding this functionality to your site takes just minutes. Many of these services also offer Google Checkout compatibility, or plan to in the near future.

account to make a purchase. Using either plan, once you've been a PayPal member for more than 90 days and have a sales volume of more than $3,000 per month, you become eligible for lower fees per transaction.

To set up this type of PayPal merchant account, call (866) 836-1648, or visit the PayPal.com website. Regardless of which plan you sign up for as a merchant, there are no setup fees and no cancellation fees. There's also no minimum contract length, which is not true of traditional credit card merchant account.

What's Next

Just because you created and launched an amazing, information-filled, easy-to-navigate, visually stunning website that offers products you know your target customers want and need doesn't mean that your potential customers will start surfing over to your site.

To generate traffic to your website will require ongoing marketing, advertising, and public relations efforts, which will take time and effort to plan and execute properly. The next chapter focuses on just some of your options for advertising, promoting, and marketing your online business, even if you're on a shoestring budget.

Chapter 9

Advertising, Promoting, and Marketing Your Online Business

*I*f you build it, they *won't* come. That is, they won't come unless you invest the time, effort, and money necessary to properly promote your online business venture and continuously drive traffic to your site. Simply publishing your e-commerce website on the internet is not enough. If people don't know about your site, the chances of their simply stumbling upon it are slim.

Sure, getting listed on the internet search engines, like Yahoo! and Google is extremely important, but it could take weeks or even months for your site to get listed and even longer to earn a good ranking, unless you pay a premium. Chapter 10 focuses on how to utilize search engine optimization and search engine marketing (aka *keyword advertising*) to generate traffic to your site.

When it comes to promoting, marketing, and advertising your online business, you have a wide range of opportunities, both in the real world and in cyberspace. Based on what you're selling and to whom you'll be selling (your target audience), you probably want to take a multifaceted approach in order to generate the most traffic to your site possible.

WARNING

As you already know, simply driving traffic to your website isn't enough. Once someone visits your site, it must contain the content and information necessary to transform that visitor into a buyer. An online business owner should always be fine-tuning his site in an effort to maximize the customer conversion rate.

Depending on a variety of factors, including what you're selling, your target audience, your budget, the amount of time you have to invest, your desired goals, and your creativity, some of the ways you can get the word out about your online business include:

➡ Paid advertising in newspapers, magazines, and newsletters, on radio and television, and in other forms of traditional media.
➡ A public relations effort designed to get the media to feature information about you (as an expert in your field), your business, and your products in articles, product reviews, feature stories, and news stories.
➡ Innovative promotions designed to appeal directly to your target audience. This might include cross-promoting your business with other businesses, sponsoring events, and coming up with unique ways of interacting in the real world with your potential customers to inform them of your business and products.

➡ Distributing marketing materials that promote your website and your business's core message. These materials could be printed catalogs, fliers, newsletters, bumper stickers, promotional T-shirts, or other giveaways with your company's name, URL, logo, and/or message imprinted on them. These materials can be distributed at trade shows, conventions, special events, and other gatherings attended by people in your target audience.

➡ Online advertising, such as paying for your display ads to appear on other websites, paying for premium placement on search engines, and the use of search engine marketing (keyword advertising).

➡ Developing online affiliates or cross-marketing programs with other websites to help drive traffic to your website.

➡ Becoming active on online chat rooms, message boards, and online special interest groups that appeal to your target customer base.

➡ Producing informational and promotional content, such as Podcasts, videos, and blogs that can be distributed using websites like YouTube (youtube.com), Yahoo Video (http://video.yahoo.com/), Google Video (http://video.google.com), and Apple iTunes (apple.com/itunes) to build awareness of your products and your business.

➡ Utilizing traditional direct mail or an opt-in e-mail list to promote your business. Whatever you do, however, stay away from sending spam (unsolicited e-mails) to potential customers. It annoys recipients and damages your business's reputation and credibility.

➡ Taking steps to generate positive word-of-mouth and soliciting referrals from existing customers. Positive word-of-mouth advertising can best be achieved by offering absolutely the best customer

CLICK TIP

Depending on what you're selling, your budget, and your target audience, you might wish to incorporate other well-established marketing, advertising, or promotional activities into your efforts. Some options include launching a telemarketing campaign, cold-calling potential customers, sponsoring some event, or using advertising billboards in major cities.

service possible and by developing a positive and ongoing relationship with all of your customers. Selling only top-quality products is also important.

The best approach when it comes to advertising, marketing, and promoting your business is to take a multifaceted approach, which means not relying on just one thing to drive traffic to your site. For example, don't just purchase a bunch of advertising space in one magazine or newspaper and expect that thousands of people will see your ad, visit your site, and become paying customers.

Likewise, don't just send out one press release to a bunch of media outlets and expect that your company and its products will receive national coverage in newspapers, in magazines, on radio, and on television.

To drive a steady flow of traffic to your online business requires you to use many different promotional, marketing, and advertising activities simultaneously on an ongoing basis. As you do this, expect that it will take time for the impact of your efforts to be seen, so make sure your expectations are realistic and that your budget is adequate to sustain your efforts.

Keep in mind that marketing, public relations, and advertising specialists spend years learning and fine-tuning their craft. Large companies spend millions of dollars using these people to advertise, market, and promote them and their products to build consumer awareness of their brand. As a startup entrepreneur trying to handle these objectives on your own, it's not realistic to expect the same results that a Fortune 500 company or established mass-market retailer would have with its multimillion dollar budget.

CLICK TIP

If you have the budget, consider hiring an experienced advertising agency, public relations firm, or marketing company to help you properly promote your online business, at least initially. Use the expertise of experienced professionals who know exactly how to pinpoint and effectively reach your target audience with an appropriate and effective advertising or marketing message. If you don't have the funds to hire an agency, consider hiring freelance advertising, marketing, and/or public relations specialists to help you design and launch your campaign.

While anyone can learn how to effectively market, promote, and advertise her own business and products, plan on experiencing a learning curve as you try different approaches to determine what works best for reaching your target audience in a cost-effective and efficient way.

No matter what approach you take creating and executing a comprehensive advertising, marketing, and promotional campaign for your business, it is going to take time and money. In fact, in the early stages of your business's operation, driving traffic to your website will probably be one of your biggest costs.

WARNING

For someone with absolutely no advertising experience, it's extremely difficult to create professional and effective ads and then know exactly where to have those ads run in order to generate the desired results. If you lack experience, you could easily throw away a large part of your advertising budget by paying to have poorly designed ads appear or paying to have well-designed ads appear in inappropriate media.

Preparing Your Advertising, Public Relations, and Marketing Campaign

The initial steps involved in creating and launching a highly effective advertising, public relations, and marketing campaign include

➡ learning everything there is to know about the product you'll be selling, including its features, key selling points, why it appeals to customers, what problems it helps to solve, how it will make the life of its user easier or better, its perceived value to the customer, and what sets it apart from the competition.

➡ determining exactly what message you're trying to convey.

➡ pinpointing the precise target audience you're trying to reach.

➡ creating ads, press releases, marketing materials, and promotional items that effectively convey your message to its intended audience.

➡ calculating the overall budget you have at your disposal.

➡ figuring out how much time you can invest in these efforts.

➡ soliciting the assistance of experienced experts.

Your next steps are to develop each facet of your overall advertising, marketing, and promotional campaign, prepare an appropriate timeline for launch, and determine how you'll accurately track the success of each element of your campaign so you can continuously fine-tune those efforts and use your budget more effectively. In other words, you need to know as quickly as possible what's working and what's not in terms of generating traffic to your site in a cost-effective manner.

CLICK TIP

During this process, learn as much as you can about advertising, marketing, and public relations fundamentals. You can do this by reading books, taking classes, or hiring experts and learning from them. You can also carefully evaluate what your competition is doing, see what works for them, and try to emulate those activities after customizing them to meet your needs.

You'll quickly discover that there is no single solution or formula for creating the perfect comprehensive campaign that will achieve your desired results. As you get to know your target customer and begin operating your business, you'll need to experiment a bit to determine which elements of your campaign are working well, which elements need to be fine-tuned, and which need to be scrapped and replaced with more efficient or cost-effective activities.

As a small startup business, your goal should be to generate the most impact through your advertising, marketing, and promotional efforts, while

CLICK TIP

Depending on the type of advertising, marketing, public relations, and promotions you do, you may be able to track the success of each component of your overall campaign immediately. It may, however, take several weeks or even months for you to be able to determine if a specific aspect of your campaign was successful. Many media outlets work on a long *lead time*. For a monthly magazine, issues are created up to three months in advance. So, if you'd like to advertise in the November issue (or use your public relations efforts to have a product review appear in that issue), you'll need to get everything set up as early as August or September.

spending the least amount of money possible. Because you can't compete dollar for dollar with mass-market retailers or other well-established businesses in terms of the money spent, you'll need to take a more grassroots, shoestring, guerrilla approach to your efforts.

Advertising Your Site

In terms of your overall marketing mix, *advertising* involves paying to have the marketing message you create, your advertisement, aired on radio or television, printed in newspapers, magazines, or other publications, or displayed online. By paying the media to run your ad or display it, you're given 100 percent control over its content. Depending on the media, this includes what it says, what it looks like, how it sounds, its size or its length, and when it's seen or heard.

Advertising certainly has its advantages in terms of being able to reach your target audience with your specific message. However, depending on where you advertise, it can also be costly. As a general rule, paid advertising requires frequency to really work. Thus, you'll need to ensure your intended audiences sees or hears your ad multiple times before you can expect them to respond by visiting your website. Running a single, 60-second radio ad or one print ad in a newspaper or magazine, for example, probably won't generate an overwhelming response.

For paid advertising to work, for you to get the most out of it based on the amount of money being spent, you must be able to reach your target audience with the right message. This requires you to brainstorm the right wording to use, the appearance of your ad (in print), or how it will sound (on radio). The ad you create is often referred to as the *creative* in the advertising industry, whether it's a print ad or a television or radio spot. The ad you create should have a well-defined goal, such as introducing your product to the public or driving people to your website to order it.

Once you've written and produced what you believe to be the perfect ad, the next step is to secure proper placement in the media; that is, when and where it will appear and how often. When you purchase advertising space or time, it's referred to as a *media buy*.

Your media buy should be with media outlets—newspapers, magazines, newsletters, radio stations, television stations, websites, or others—that allow you to reach your target audience. If you're trying to reach women between the ages of 18 and 49, for example, advertising in a men's magazine, whether it's *GQ, Details, Sports Illustrated,* or *Playboy,* would be absolutely pointless.

Part of being a successful advertiser involves finding media outlets that you can afford and that will allow you to reach your target audience as effectively as possible. Typically, when you're paying for advertising, the more advertising space or time you purchase, the greater the discount you're given. The advertising rates you pay are often highly negotiable.

Start by pinpointing what media outlets you'd benefit from advertising in. Next, determine the cost associated with creating the ad you wish to run. You then need to contact each appropriate media outlet's advertising department and request a media kit, which will include advertising rates, ad specifications, and information about the media outlet. Based on the price list and information in the media kit, you can determine if running your ad with that outlet is affordable and conducive to achieving your desired results.

If your business will be selling a very specialized or niche product to a specific audience, you want to find special interest publications that cater to that unique audience. While running an ad in a general interest magazine such as *Time, Newsweek, US Weekly,* or *People* allows you to reach millions of readers, how many of them actually fit into your target demographic? If it's only 5 or 10 percent of the readers, spending tens of thousands of dollars (or more) to run that ad in a general interest magazine is pointless. You're paying to reach too many people you already know have no interest in what you're selling.

CLICK TIP

When you run an ad, you want to determine how many people overall will be exposed to it. This is the number of "impressions" your ad will make. From those impressions, you then want to determine how many responses you receive, for example, how many people saw or heard your ad and immediately visited your website. Another important statistic to track is how many people placed an order for your product based on the number of visitors to your site as a result of seeing or hearing your ad. Ultimately, it's the orders generated that increase your business's revenues. Paying for ads that don't generate enough sales or a high enough response rate is pointless.

Instead, it makes more sense to find a special interest publication that may only have a circulation of 5,000 but with 80 to 90 percent of those readers who are part of your target audience.

Pinpointing the best media outlets to advertise with, whether print (newspapers, magazines, newsletters, etc.), electronic (radio or television), or online (websites or search engines), will play a tremendous role in your success and determine what type of response you receive from an ad.

In addition to creating the perfect ad and then selecting the most appropriate media to showcase it, all advertisers face the challenge of making their ad stand out from the others. As consumers, we're trained to tune out advertising. As an advertiser, however, your goal is to create an ad (or series of ads) that captures peoples' attention. Accomplishing this requires creativity.

If you read a newspaper, how many ads do you actually take more than a few seconds to glance at? What about the ads in the magazines you read? How much time do you spend glancing at each of them before turning the page? Typically, it's only a few brief seconds. As the advertiser, your goal must be to capture the reader's attention in that brief time and ensure your ad doesn't get totally lost among the other ads in the publication.

If you're advertising on radio or television, you only have that same few seconds to capture people's attention before they switch stations, walk away from their television for a snack, or engage in some other activity that distracts them until their programming returns. With so many things to consider when creating and executing an advertising campaign, make sure your initial expectations are realistic. Expect to make some mistakes early on, and

---

CLICK TIP

When selecting appropriate media outlets to advertise with, focus on reaching your target audience in a cost-effective way. Figure out how you can spend the least amount of money to reach the largest number of people in your target audience, which often involves advertising in a handful of different media. Because you're paying to place your ads and you have total control over the content, it's essential that your ads communicate the most compelling message possible as quickly as possible in order to generate the best response rate.

be prepared to fine-tune your campaign until the ad message and the ad placement is right, based on what you're selling and to whom you're selling it.

Public Relations 101

Public relations involves working with the same media outlets you might advertise with, but in a very different way. Using public relations strategies, your goal is to work with reporters, writers, editors, and journalists to convince them to include information about you, your company, and your products in their editorial content.

This might mean getting interviewed as an expert in your field as part of a news story, having your product featured in a review, or having your product included in the news, features, or human interest stories that make up the editorial content of newspapers, magazines, radio shows, and television talk shows and news programs.

When you use public relations, you provide reporters, writers, editors, and journalists with the information they need for their articles or stories. However, you have absolutely no control over what's written or said about your products or your company. You run the risk that details about your product will be misrepresented or that important details will be left out.

The benefit of public relations, however, is that when you, your company, and/or your product are featured in various media outlets it doesn't cost you a penny. In addition, when readers, listeners, or viewers hear about your product from a reporter or journalist they trust, they're more apt to buy the product or visit your website than they would if they merely saw or heard an ad.

The trick to generating positive and free publicity is to develop relationships with those who currently reach your target audience. This relationship can be established by sending a detailed press kit or press releases about your company and its products, and, if applicable, providing a sample of the product for the reporters, writers, editors, and journalists to test or review firsthand.

CLICK TIP

To learn how to write and format a press release, visit one of these websites: publicityinsider.com/release.asp, press-release-writing.com/10_essential_tips.htm, internetbased moms.com/press-releases, or wikihow .com/Write-a-Press-Release.

Every day, media figures are bombarded with dozens, sometimes hundreds, of press releases and press kits. Thus, the information you provide must adhere to a specific format, be comprehensive, be of interest, and be timely. You must also take into account the lead time people in the media work under and be conscious of their often tight deadlines. The easier it is to include information about you,

CLICK TIP

In addition to creating printed copies of your press materials that can be mailed to targeted media, you also want to create a Press, Press Room, or Media area on your website that contains these materials and makes them available for downloading by members of the media.

your company, and/or your product in their articles, features, reviews, or segments, the better your chances of receiving the free media coverage you're seeking.

Like advertising, planning and executing an effective public relations campaign takes skill, creativity, experience, and the ability to capture the attention of reporters, writers, editors, and journalists in a positive way. If done correctly, being featured in a single newspaper, in a magazine article, on radio, or on television can easily generate a better response than spending tens of thousands of dollars on paid advertising. Once the publicity appears in the media, you'll see immediate results in the form of additional traffic to your site.

The best way to begin to generate free publicity is with a well-written press release about your company and/or product. This press release must adhere to a standard press release format, contain a newsworthy message, be well written, and contain all of the information the recipient needs to know.

CLICK TIP

By positioning yourself as an expert in your field, you could be invited to be interviewed by the news media as part of a timely story that relates to your area of expertise. Or, you could be invited to be a guest on a talk radio show or television talk show. As a guest being interviewed, you can plug your products, direct people to your website, and build credibility with the audience.

Answer the questions who, what, where, when, why, and how. A typical press release is double-spaced and fits on one or two pages.

A press kit is a folder that contains several specific press releases about your product, along with a one- or two-page company backgrounder, short biographies of company executives, product photos, and copies of press clippings already generated.

If you've never written a press release or put together a press kit, consider hiring a freelance public relations specialist or a PR firm to assist you. Being able to determine exactly what information a member of the media will want or need—and presenting that information to them properly—is essential.

After your press materials are created, the next step is to compile a list of specific reporters, writers, editors, and journalists, based on their beats, that is, the topics they typically report on or write about. This is your customized media list. If your online business involves selling handcrafted sweaters for infants, it's important to target only journalists that cover parenting topics or crafts, for example. In other words, don't approach sports reporters or entertainment reporters.

There are several ways to track down the right people to send your press materials to, but first you need to create a list of media outlets you want to target in hopes of generating publicity. Next, contact each one to obtain the name, title, address, phone number, and e-mail address of the appropriate reporter, writer, editor, or journalist. An alternative is to use a comprehensive media directory that lists this information.

Bacon's Media Directories (866-639-5087, http://us.cision.com/products _services/bacons_media_directories_2008.asp) provide a comprehensive listing of all newspapers, magazines, radio stations, and television stations, along with contacts at each one. The printed directories are updated annually, and a complete media database is also available online for a fee. Several other companies offer similar directories and databases. They include:

➡ *The Gebbie Press All-In-One Media Directory*—gebbie.com, (845) 255-7560
➡ *Media Contacts Pro*—mediacontactspro.com/products.php, (800) 351-1383
➡ *Burrelles/Luce*—burrellsluce.com/MediaContacts, (800) 368-8070

The reference section of your public library may be a good resource for these directories.

CLICK TIP

To save time and potentially money once your press release is written, you can pay a press release distribution service, such as PR Newswire (prnewswire.com) to distribute it electronically, via fax, or by U.S. mail to the media contacts you identify. Within hours, thousands of reporters, writers, editors, and journalists could have information about you, your company, and your products waiting in their inbox.

To save money when compiling your media list, consider visiting a large newsstand, looking through the newspapers and magazines, and then checking the masthead of each appropriate publication for the proper contact details. You can also review the ending credits of television talk shows and news programs, and contact news and talk radio stations.

Mastering the art of working with the media to generate free publicity can be an extremely cost-effective way to promote your business and build its positive reputation on the local, regional, national, or even international level if you're on a shoestring budget. It can also be an extremely powerful tool if used correctly, and should definitely be a prominent part of your overall marketing/advertising campaign for your business. You'll find that once you start generating positive publicity, other media outlets will start featuring you, your company, or your products in their editorial coverage.

Figure 9.1 on page 120 is a sample press released provided by KielJames Patrick.com, which showcases a typical press release format, as well as the type of content to include within a press release when announcing a new e-commerce business.

Remember, the format of your press release is as important as its content if you want to capture the attention of an editor, journalist, producer, or reporter. To learn more about Kiel James Patrick, see the in-depth interview featured within Chapter 12 of this book.

Figure 9.2 on page 122 is a sample company background information sheet (also referred to as a backgrounder) provided by KielJamesPatrick.com. It showcases the type of information that can be incorporated into this type of document in order to educate the media and potential customers about a company.

Figure 9.1: **SAMPLE PRESS RELEASE**

Kiel James Patrick Custom Wristbands:
Something Old Has Launch an Exciting New, Trendy, and Premium Brand
kieljamespatrick.com

For Immediate Release   Contact: [Insert Name]

[Insert Phone Number]

[Insert E-mail Address]

Cranston, Rhode Island—Kiel James Patrick, a 25-year-old entrepreneur and veteran fashion model, has launched a premium fashion accessory brand that specializes in creating custom-designed, irregularly stitched wristbands made from fabrics recycled from vintage neckties.

Available exclusively from the company's own website (kieljamespatrick.com), as well as select upscale boutiques in Los Angeles, Rhode Island, and Boston, the Kiel James Patrick® Wristbands represent the newest all-American collegiate accessory that has fashion-focused males and females alike clamoring to wrap their wrists in one or more of these truly unique accessory items.

"Since launching the KJP website in February 2008, we've literally been bombarded with orders from high school and college students, young professionals, and even a handful of Hollywood celebrities, including well-known actors, recording artists, and models. This has quickly become the fashion accessory item people want to be seen wearing in all of the hottest nightclubs, in the classroom, and in the workplace. The wristbands are stylish and custom-designed to reflect the wearer's unique personality," said Patrick.

From the company's website, customers select their favorite vintage material (which comes from recycled neckties acquired from secondhand shops and other sources), and then chooses an intricately designed button which serves as the wristband's fastener. There are dozens of fashionable fabrics to choose from, with new styles slated to be released each season. After selecting a size and placing their order, each wristband is handmade in Cranston, Rhode Island, and shipped to the customer within 48 hours.

"We also have in-store displays at a growing number of select, up-scale fashion boutiques that display about 45 of our most popular styles and colors, allowing customers

Figure 9.1: **SAMPLE PRESS RELEASE,** CONTINUED

to purchase and wear their favorite KJP wristband immediately," added Patrick, who is proud that his creations are able to showcase the timeless style of all American youth.

Prices for the one-of-a-kind KJP wristbands range from $30 to $90 each, depending on the vintage fabric style, and the unique, oversized, customized button (bearing the company's logo) that's selected. The interior of each band is lined with Kiel James Patrick's signature plaid fabric.

"Vintage men's neckties come in all sorts of fabrics, colors, and styles. By reworking these old ties and combining them with classic, custom-designed, oversize buttons— currently available in silver, bronze, and a handful of other finishes—we've created extremely stylish, modern, and comfortable fashion accessories that can be worn alone or in groups of two or three on a single wrist," explained Patrick.

Within weeks of the website's launch, Patrick has been contacted by several Hollywood stylists looking to accessorize their celebrity clients and even incorporate the wristbands into on-screen wardrobes to be seen on popular TV shows. "It's truly become a fashion phenomenon," he added.

Additional information about the KJP wristbands can be obtained at the company's website (kieljamespatrick.com), or by calling (###) ###-####. Kiel James Patrick is currently available for interviews and photo shoots. High-resolution product photographs, along with product samples, are available to the media upon request.

# # #

If you visit the KJP website, you'll find this background information prominently displayed online. A printed version was also sent to more than 100 fashion magazines, websites, and blogs, along with a sample of the company's product and a press release, in order to generate publicity for the company and the KJP website.

To learn more about Kiel James Patrick, see the in-depth interview featured within Chapter 12 of this book.

Figure 9.2: COMPANY BACKGROUND INFORMATION

Kiel James Patrick
Company Backgrounder
kieljamespatrick.com

A native of Cranston, Rhode Island, 25-year-old **Kiel James Patrick** is a veteran fashion model and an entrepreneur who recently launched his own fashion accessory brand and product line.

Available exclusively from the company's own website (**kieljamespatrick.com**), as well as from select upscale fashion boutiques, the Kiel James Patrick (KJP) wristbands are handcrafted, irregularly stitched, stylish, and unique creations made from recycled vintage neckties (and other vintage fabrics), and combined with a custom-designed and logoed button which fastens the wristband around the wearer's wrist.

The KJP wristbands represent the newest, all-American collegiate accessory that has fashion-focused males and females alike clamoring to wrap their wrists in one or more of these unique accessory items. In fact, not only have these wristbands instantly become a "must have" accessory item in high schools and on college campuses, they've also achieved tremendous popularity amongst nightclub goers and Hollywood celebrities.

"The first question people ask me when they see a Kiel James Patrick wristband is, 'How did you come up with the idea?' Well, it all began back in 2004, while I was rifling through an antique chest in the attic that contained some of my grandfather's old neckties. I really admired the traditional patterns and designs, and realized how much our current styles lacked personality," explained Patrick. "I started wearing a few of the ties and decided to cut one up and stitch the frayed ends, in order to transform it into a wristband."

For an entire year while in school, Patrick wore his original bracelet. Time after time, his friends and people he met kept asking where they could buy one for themselves. As his friends continued requesting wristbands, Patrick quickly needed to obtain more vintage

Figure 9.2: **COMPANY BACKGROUND INFORMATION,** CONTINUED

materials. "This led to a journey across New England to accumulate a vast quantity of quality vintage fabrics. I loved the attention I was getting, and would gladly create a bracelet for anyone who asked. I relished that people thought so highly of my personal fashion concept. Eventually, I realized I should make my bracelets available to the public," he added.

"My brand of wristbands caters directly to the public's need for individuality and uniqueness," added Patrick. Visitors to the company's website can choose from dozens of vintage fabrics, and then select one of several different custom-designed and over-sized KJP buttons (which fastens the bracelet), so each wristband is custom-created, one-of-a-kind, and handmade to reflect the wearer's own personality. Orders placed on the website are created and shipped within 48 hours.

Prices for the KJP wristbands range between $30 and $90, depending on the vintage fabric style and the customized button (bearing the company's logo) that's selected. The interior of each band is lined with Kiel James Patrick's signature plaid fabric. The availability of styles, vintage fabrics, and color schemes will change with each season.

For the upscale fashion boutiques that have already placed wholesale orders to sell the wristbands, Patrick has designed a wooden in-store display that holds approximately 45

of the most popular wristband styles, allowing customers to purchase and wear their favorite KJP wristband immediately.

"People are wearing the wristbands with the oversize KJP logoed button facing either up or down, it doesn't matter. The style really works when someone wears two or three bracelets together on one wrist. They're designed to be timeless and promote an all-American look. The wristbands can be worn with virtually any outfit, from jeans and a T-shirt, to business casual attire, or something you'd wear to a nightclub or for brunch at the

Figure 9.2: **COMPANY BACKGROUND INFORMATION,** CONTINUED

country club," said Patrick. "Guys and girls of all ages, and from all walks of life are wearing the wristbands."

Kiel James Patrick launched his company's website in mid-February 2008, and simultaneously kicked off a grassroots marketing campaign using MySpace.com and Facebook.com to reach his target audience.

"Word-of-mouth has spread extremely quickly," he stated proudly. "We've been receiving orders from across the country, as well as from several celebrities and a few Hollywood stylists who have expressed a strong interest in incorporating my wristbands into wardrobe to be worn on popular television shows. The response has been truly beyond my wildest expectations."

For additional information about Kiel James Patrick wristbands, or to place an order, visit the company's website at kieljamespatrick.com. Wholesale inquiries are invited.

# # #

Marketing Strategies

Marketing for your online business can mean many different things and encompass a wide range of activities—from establishing top-notch customer service in your organization so your customers provide positive word-of-mouth advertising for your products to sponsoring a Little League team in your city and having your website URL displayed on the players' uniforms.

You can also effectively market your online business by producing and distributing informational or instructional podcasts or videos and distributing them via services like You Tube, or by publishing a newsletter or blog that you distribute free of charge to people that opt in your e-mail list.

By producing informational or how-to content that you distribute free of charge to prospective customers as well as to your existing customers, you are providing them with content they see as valuable. In exchange, these people are willing to give you their e-mail address or mailing address, and allow you

CLICK TIP

To learn more about podcasting and how to get started using pod-casting as a marketing tool for your business, visit any of these websites: http://en.wikipedia.org/wiki/Podcasting, bswusa.com/podcast.asp, podcast.net, podcasting-tools.com, or podcastingnews.com/articles/What_is_Podcasting.html.

to share with them some marketing or advertising materials about your company and its products.

While your daily, weekly, or monthly podcast, video, newsletter, or blog, for example, should contain information of interest to the audience, it can also contain subtle marketing messages that promote your business and its products. Using these tools allows you to build credibility, enhance company or brand awareness, and generate interest in your products in an informal way.

E-mailing your electronic newsletter to people who have subscribed to it or who have asked to be added to your opt-in mailing list can be a powerful way to catch someone's attention and communicate information. It's very different from sending unsolicited, spam e-mails to people who never requested contact with you or your business.

By posting an informative blog that gets regularly updated as part of your site (daily, weekly, or monthly), you'll be inviting your customers to keep returning, which may translate into more sales. To learn more about blogging and how it can be used as a powerful marketing tool, visit blogger.com, blog.com, typepad.com, or http://en.wikipedia.org/wiki/Blog.

Another time-tested marketing strategy involves having your logo, website URL, and marketing message imprinted on giveaway items, such as T-shirts,

CLICK TIP

As with any type of advertising, promotion, or marketing, what you opt to do should be cost-effective, target your audience, and allow you to communicate your marketing message in ways that are suitable for what you're selling and to whom you're selling.

hats, buttons, pens, or bumper stickers, for example, and then distributing the giveaways to your potential customers for free. This can be done at special events, at trade shows or conventions, or by mailings to current or potential customers.

What's Next

This chapter provided only the briefest of introductions to the many different ways you can advertise, market, and promote your online business and the product you plan to sell. As an online business operator, however, one of the most powerful advertising and promotional tools available to you is the internet itself.

The next chapter focuses specifically on search engine optimization (how to get listed on the various search engines and receive a high ranking) and on keyword advertising, which has become one of the most cost-efficient and powerful ways to drive traffic to almost any type of website.

Even if you forego other marketing and advertising methods, you want to drive traffic to your site and reach people who are already on the internet and in search of what you're selling. So, you definitely want to use search engine optimization and keyword advertising. The results will be more positive than many other types of paid advertising, including online banner or online display advertising.

After all, when web surfers are looking for just about anything online, the place they usually start their search is a search engine or web directory, such as Google.com, Yahoo.com, Ask.com, Hotbot.com, Altavista.com, or AOL Search.com. Thus, it's in your online business's best interest to be prominently featured on these sites when someone enters a keyword or search phrase that somehow relates to your company or its products.

Chapter 10

Search Engine Optimization and Marketing

*O*nce your site is online and you're ready for business, one of your ongoing challenges will be to drive ample traffic to your site and then transform those visitors into paying customers who buy the product you're selling. In the last chapter, you learned about the importance of traditional advertising, marketing, promotions, and public relations in building awareness of your site.

In this chapter, the focus is on online advertising and marketing opportunities that drive web surfers to your site when they're activity looking for your product.

Regardless of what you're selling, a comprehensive, well-planned online marketing and advertising campaign might include:

➡ *Ongoing search engine optimization (SEO).* This involves getting your site listed with the major search engines, such as Yahoo! and Google, and then working to maintain and improve your ranking/positioning with each search engine so your site is easy to find and receives top placement.

➡ *Search engine marketing.* This involves paid, keyword (text-based) advertising using Yahoo Search Engine Marketing, Google AdWords, and/or Microsoft AdCenter. This marketing helps to drive very targeted traffic to your site easily and inexpensively. These short, text-only ads are keyword based and appear when a potential customer enters a specific search phrase into a search engine.

➡ *Online display advertising.* Instead of using just text, display ads, including banner ads, allow you to use graphics, animation, and even sound or video to capture the attention of potential customers as they surf the web. Online display advertising has some advantages, but it's usually much more costly than search engine marketing and not always as effective. Like traditional print ads, display ads often get ignored.

➡ *Affiliate marketing.* This marketing plan involves getting other online merchants and websites that are not direct competitors but appeal to your target market to promote your online business by displaying ads or offering links to your site on theirs. In exchange, you pay that site on either a per-view or per-click basis, or offer a commission on any sales that site helps generate through a referral.

CLICK TIP

Search engine optimization efforts are an absolute must for all online entrepreneurs, because they allow you to drive traffic to your site when potential customers are online and in the process of looking for your product using a search engine. Realistically, it takes several weeks after you've completed the registration process for your site to start showing up on search engines.

CLICK TIP

As with traditional forms of advertising and marketing, your creativity and how well you know your customer base and product play a tremendous role in how successful your efforts are. When using search engine marketing, for example, it is up to you to compile a comprehensive list of keywords that pertain to your listing so when someone enters one or more of those words into a search engine, details about your website are displayed. The right combination of keywords generates well-qualified traffic to your site. The wrong list of keywords generates waste in your advertising and marketing budget.

Whatever methods you adopt to promote your business using online marketing/advertising tools, they should be ongoing. You should also keep constant tabs on all of them. Finally, each thing you do should be part of an overall, multifaceted campaign.

As you proceed, you'll want to tinker with your campaign regularly based on the results generated. You need to determine exactly what works and what doesn't. Then, fine-tune your efforts periodically to ensure you're attracting the most qualified traffic possible for the least amount of advertising money possible.

The online marketing and advertising methods described in this chapter work well for virtually any type of online business because they're able to reach potential customers while the surfers are visiting a search engine and using keywords specifically to find the product you're selling. This makes them pre-qualified potential customers, people who are probably ready to make a purchase online, assuming you can offer them what they're looking for at the right price. To get the sale, however, your website must also offer a professional look as well as the functionality and ease of use necessary to quickly establish a web surfer's confidence in your business.

Help Surfers Find Your Biz Using Search Engine Optimization (SEO)

When more than 80 percent of all web surfers want to find something online, whether it's a tidbit of information, a particular website, or some type of specialized content, the place they begin (if they don't already know the URL address for the website they're looking for) is at a search engine.

There are hundreds of search engines and web directories available to web surfers. The most popular of which are Google and Yahoo!, followed by MSN.com, ASK.com, AOLSearch.com, and AltaVista.com.

Your goal as an online business owner is first to get your website's URL listed with each of the major search engines, and then to work toward optimizing your listing so it receives the best ranking and placement possible. After all, if you're in the balloon delivery business and someone enters the search phrase, "Balloon Delivery, New York City" into Google, several dozen or perhaps hundreds of relevant listings will probably show up. A typical web surfer will visit the first listing and maybe the second and/or third for price comparison purposes. But, all subsequent listings will be ignored. This is why earning a top placement or ranking with each search engine is essential for driving traffic to your site.

CLICK TIP

When it comes to hiring a company to help with your business's search engine optimization, there are hundreds of choices. You want to compare prices as well as services offered. For example, will the submission service simply get your website listed with the search engines or will it take added steps to earn you excellent placement or a top ranking? Will the service evaluate your site to make sure its HTML programming and content will generate the best results with the search engines? You'll also need to determine if the service keeps your listing up to date on an ongoing basis and whether updating costs extra.

Incorporating Meta Tags into Your Website's HTML Programming

In addition to accepting submissions from website operators, many search engines and web directories use automated spiders or crawlers to continuously search the entire World Wide Web and gather details about new websites (and updates to existing sites) to list. How these automatic listings are gathered, cataloged, and categorized is based in large part on how your website utilizes *meta tags* and keywords throughout the site.

Meta tags have three parts: 1) the title of your site, 2) a description, and 3) a list of keywords. The information you provide (by incorporating it into your site's HTML programming) is then used to categorize your site's content appropriately. In addition to the site's description, title, and a list of relevant keywords within the HTML programming of

CLICK TIP

Meta tags can be easily and quickly incorporated into the HTML programming of any website. When you utilize a complete e-commerce turnkey solution, it is often done on your behalf.

your site, you'll need to incorporate a text-based, one-line *description* of your site, which again utilizes keywords to describe your site's content.

The more well thought out and comprehensive your meta tags are, the more traffic you'll generate to your site once it gets added to a search engine. If your e-commerce turnkey solution doesn't automatically incorporate meta tags into your website, there are many free online tools that allow you to create them and the appropriate HTML programming, and then cut-and-paste these lines of programming into your site with ease. No programming knowledge is required.

If you need help creating meta tags, use any search engine and enter the search phrase "Meta Tag Creation," for example, or visit one of these websites:

- ➡ ineedhits.com/free-tools/free-metatags.aspx
- ➡ scrubtheweb.com/abs/builder.html
- ➡ anybrowser.com/MetaTagGenerator.html
- ➡ yooter.com/meta.php
- ➡ funender.com/phpBB2/meta_tag_creator.php

WARNING

When creating your keyword list for your site's meta tags and description, create a comprehensive list that's relevant to your site's content but avoid excessive repetition of keywords and phrases. The search engine spiders identify repetition and hold this attempt at deception against you when cataloging and listing your site.

Step 1: List Your Site with the Popular Search Engines

As soon as your website is published, or posted, on the web, you want to begin the process of listing it with the search engines and web directories. One way to speed up the process is to pay each popular search engine for premium placement, (covered later in this chapter).

CLICK TIP

As the content of your website evolves and grows, be sure to update your meta tags to reflect this additional content. Keep in mind that it could take weeks for your updates to be reflected on the individual search engines.

Why list your site with the search engines? Well, the answer is simple. Most web surfers begin their search for specific content from a search engine. They enter keywords or phrases, and then they follow the first few links provided by the search engine to reach the sites that potentially interest them. If someone is looking for the product you're selling and enters in a keyword that describes that product, he will be able to find you quickly and easily when your website is listed with the search engines.

Search engines and web directories are like telephone books where people can look up listings based on keywords or phrases. There are literally thousands of search engines and web directories on the internet, but the majority of web surfers mainly use the most popular search engines, so it's essential that your site is represented on these sites.

The cheapest way to get your site listed with the search engines is to visit each one yourself and complete the new listing submission form. This process is free. It involves completing a brief questionnaire that helps the search engine find, catalog, and categorize your proposed listing. It's important to understand that the listing submission process is different for each search engine and web directory. Once you've completed the process, it will be necessary to update your listing periodically in order to maintain and improve your ranking or position.

CLICK TIP

While it's not necessary to get listed on every single search engine, your goal should be to obtain highly ranked listings on the most trafficked and most popular search engines, such as Yahoo! and Google in order to reach the greatest number of people.

When listing your site with some of the search engines and web directories, the process is as simple as entering the URL address and title of your site. The listing and submission process for other search engines, however, is much more in-depth and must be done correctly. In some cases, your site will need to get approved by a human before it is listed.

CLICK TIP

A comprehensive introduction to search engine marketing and search engine submissions can be found at the Search Engine Watch website (http://search enginewatch.com/showPage.html?page=web masters).

The following links can be used to submit a listing for your new website on some of the most popular search engines and web directories:

- Google—google.com/addurl
- Yahoo!—https://siteexplorer.search.yahoo.com/submit
- MSN Live Search—http://search.msn.com/docs/submit.aspx
- Ask—countrystarsonline.com/jimweaver/submit/askjeeves.htm
- AltaVista—altavista.com/addurl/default

A quicker, but more expensive way, to get your site listed with the popular search engines is to pay a third-party submission service, such as Go Daddy.com's Traffic Blazer, to handle the process on your behalf. If you opt to use one of these services, be sure you understand exactly what you're paying for and what results you can realistically expect. For example, if you pay a service $39.95 to list your site on hundreds of the major search engines, chances are this will include a listing, but not guarantee prominent placement.

To earn a high ranking or prominent placement on a search engine takes human intervention when submitting a listing, and when programming your website, in order to provide exactly the information the search engines look for in the site's HTML programming and meta tags. An inexpensive auto-mated submission process does not typically guarantee top-ranked listings.

Step 2: Focus on Improving Your Site's Ranking and Position

After your site gets listed with a search engine and appears when searches are conducted, it then becomes your responsibility to keep your listing up to date and take whatever steps necessary to maintain and improve your listing. This activity is referred to as *search engine optimization* because your objective is to optimize the placement or ranking of your search.

Again, this is a time-consuming process you can do yourself. You can also hire a SEO expert to handle it on your behalf, which will probably generate better results faster. If you want or need to have a listing for your site appear on the search engines quickly (within hours, not weeks), seriously consider using paid search engine marketing through Yahoo!, Microsoft, and/or Google AdWords to supplement your free listings.

If you have a good budget, you can also use display advertising and web-site sponsorships to ensure that your message gets communicated to web surfers.

Search Engine Optimization Tools and Resources

To find a third-party company that specializes is submitting URL listings to search engines as well as search engine optimization enter the search phrases "search engine submissions" or "search engine optimization" into any search engine. You'll discover hundreds, potentially thousands, of paid services you can use, including:

➡ buildtraffic.com/indexnew.shtml
➡ engineseeker.com
➡ godaddy.com/gdshop/traffic_blazer/landing.asp
➡ iclimber.com
➡ networksolutions.com/online-marketing/index.jsp
➡ seop.com
➡ submitasite.com
➡ toprankresults.com
➡ trafficxs.com/platinum.htm

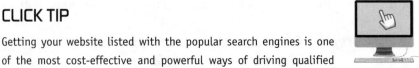

CLICK TIP

Getting your website listed with the popular search engines is one of the most cost-effective and powerful ways of driving qualified traffic to your website. This should be a priority when planning and then implementing your company's overall marketing, advertising, promotional, and public relations efforts.

➡ worldsubmit.com
➡ wpromote.com/quicklist/landing

Drive Targeted Traffic to Your Site Using Search Engine Marketing

It used to be that the most cost-effective, quickest, and easiest ways to drive traffic to your website was to use online banner ads (display ads). These ads could be purchased to appear on websites that catered to the same audience or demographic the advertiser was attempting to reach. However, as web surfers have become more savvy and less patient, this is no longer the case. While display ads can still work and help build brand awareness, if your goal is to drive traffic to your website through the use of online advertising and marketing, search engine optimization and search engine marketing are currently the best ways to go, regardless of what you're selling.

Whenever you visit one of the popular search engines, and many other websites, including blogs, you'll notice short, text-based ads displayed on the page that are directly relevant to what you're searching for or to the content on the site you're currently visiting. For example, if you've done a search about Yorkshire Terrier puppies, the paid, text-based ads you'll see displayed will relate directly to dogs and/or Yorkshire Terriers.

These text-based ads are paid for by advertisers using one of several services, including:

➡ *Yahoo! Search Engine Marketing*– http://sem.smallbusiness.yahoo.com/searchenginemarketing, (866) 747-7327
➡ *Google AdWords*–http://adwords.google.com
➡ *Microsoft AdCenter*–http://advertising.microsoft.com/search-advertising

Search engine marketing has a number of benefits to the advertiser, including:

➡ It's extremely inexpensive to launch a search engine marketing ad campaign. The initial investment is typically under $50, and you have 100 percent control over your daily ad spending. Once you set your budget, you pay only for the actual clicks to your site, not the impressions (people who see your ad).
➡ You can create and launch a fully customized search engine marketing campaign in just minutes and start seeing results within hours.

➡ The success of your campaign depends on your ability to select appropriate and relevant keywords that are being used by web surfers to find specific content.

➡ You can track the success of your campaign in real time, using online tools provided by Yahoo!, Google, and/or Microsoft when you use their services.

➡ Your ad campaign can be expanded as you achieve success and generate a profit, or it can be modified or cancelled in minutes (not weeks or months) to address changes in your overall marketing campaign or your company's objectives.

Launch Your Search Engine Marketing Ad Campaign

The first step in launching a search engine marketing campaign is to choose the service or services you'll use. Yahoo! Small Business' Search Engine Marketing, Google AdWords, or Microsoft AdCenter are the most popular. If you opt to use Google AdWords, for example, your ads will appear on Google whenever someone enters a search phrase that matches the keywords you select in your ad (providing you're willing to pay the going rate for that ad to be displayed—a concept that will be explained shortly).

In addition to Google AdWords ads being displayed through Google's own search engine site, the company has partnered with thousands of other websites and blog operators that also display context-sensitive ads through the AdWords service. This is the Google AdWords' content network, and it includes About.com, Lycos.com, FoodNetwork.com, *The New York Times* On The Web, InfoSpace, Business.com, HowStuffWorks.com, and literally thousands of other sites around the world.

In fact, according to Google, "The Google content network reaches 75 percent of unique internet users in more than 20 languages and over 100 counties. As a result, if you advertise on both the Google search network and the Google content network, you have the potential to reach three of every four unique internet users on Earth."

Yahoo! and Microsoft have similar content networks that allow targeted, text-based ads to be displayed on a wide range of websites well beyond each company's primary search engine or web directory. As you compare the search engine marketing programs offered by these companies, not only will you want to compare rates, you'll also want to determine if each company's content network will help you reach your target audience.

Once you choose which company or companies you'd like to advertise with, the process of launching your campaign involves a few simple steps:

1. Set up an account with the search engine marketing company you'd like to work with. This requires the use of a credit card, debit card, or PayPal account, and a deposit of about $50 to get started. (The deposit varies among the various services.)

2. Create a detailed list of keywords that relates directly to the product your business sells. These keywords can include industry jargon, product names, your company's name, and any other keywords you deem relevant.

3. Create a text-based ad. Each ad includes a headline, a short body, and URL that links directly to your website.

4. Decide on how much you'd like to spend on your campaign each day. Part of this decision is deciding how much you're willing to pay each time someone sees your ad and clicks on it in order to reach your website. With this type of advertising, you do not pay for the number of impressions the ad receives. You only pay each time someone actually clicks on the link to visit your website. Based on the keywords you select, you'll be competing with other companies running ads with similar keywords. Using a complex formula that takes into account how much you're willing to pay-per-click, your ad's placement and the frequency each is displayed will be determined. The more you are willing to pay per-click, especially for popular keywords, the better your ad placement will be and the more frequently it will be viewed by web surfers using those keywords to find what they're looking for. Thus, when you launch your campaign, you must set a maximum cost-per-click as well as a total daily spending limit, which can be as little as $10 per day.

5. As you create your search engine marketing campaign, you can determine who sees your ad based on geographic location.

6. To help you create a comprehensive and effective list of keywords, the search engine marketing services (operated by Yahoo!, Google, and Microsoft, among others) offer a set of online tools to help you create your ad's keyword list and forecast how many impressions your ad will receive based on your ad budget.

7. Once your ad campaign is running, you can use online tools to keep tabs on the number of overall impressions, click-throughs, ad placement, ad positioning, and related costs. This tracking is done in real time, so you know instantly if your campaign is working.

CLICK TIP

According to Yahoo!, in July 2007, "Over 2.3 billion searches occur on Yahoo! each month. Prospective customers could be searching for what your business sells right now! Geographic targeting enables you to target your advertising to customers in your area or across the country." According to Microsoft, "We reach more than 465 million unique consumers each month globally, and 117 million in the United States."

As you create your search engine marketing campaign, you'll come across a handful of advertising-related terms, including:

➡ *Click-through-rate (CTR)*. Refers to the number of clicks your website receives as a result of someone clicking on an ad divided by the total number of impressions (views) the ad received.

➡ *Cost-per-click (CPC)*. A number that refers to the total cost of running the ad campaign, divided by the number of clicks to your site that you receive. The goal is for this number to be as low as possible. For example, if you pay $100 for a campaign that generates 10 hits, your CPC is $10 each. However, if that same $100 campaign generates 1,000 hits, your CPS is just $ .10 each.

➡ *Display URL*. The URL for your website that's actually displayed in your search engine marketing ad. In reality, you can have the ad link to any URL or any HTML page within your domain. If the Display URL is SampleSite.com, in reality, the link could lead a surfer to SampleSite.com/ProductInfo.htm.

➡ *Keyword*. A specific word or phrase that relates to a product, a company, or any content on your website that you're advertising or promoting. If you are using search engine marketing, your text-based ad could be displayed when someone uses the search phrase that matches your keyword.

A complete glossary of terms can be found at Yahoo!'s website (https://signup13.marketingsolutions.yahoo.com/signupui/signup/glossary.do) as well as at the end of this book. Understanding these terms will help you better utilize the advertising tools that are at your disposal.

The Anatomy of a Search Engine Marketing Ad

Some reasons why text-based search engine marketing ads work so well are the ads that appear for each web surfer are always directly relevant to the topic she's actively seeking. The ads are very short and to the point, and the ads serve as links directly to websites that have the content the surfer is looking for at that very moment. From the advertiser's standpoint, this type of advertising can be extremely targeted by region and/or by keywords. Thus, these ads can quickly and efficiently pre-qualify a potential customer and attract them to your site at the precise moment she's looking for what your site offers.

In addition to ensuring your ads get the best possible placement on the search engine websites, as well as throughout the appropriate websites within the search engine marketing company's content network, it's your responsibility as the advertiser to create a short, text-based ad that quickly captures the reader's attention and generates enough excitement for them to click on your link.

Creating an effective search engine marketing ad takes creativity as well as a strong knowledge of your product and target audience. What you say in your ad must be relevant, appealing, and attention getting. However, you have relatively little space to accomplish this rather significant task.

Regardless of whether you use Yahoo Search Engine Marketing, Google AdWords, Microsoft AdCenter, or another service, the anatomy of the ad that web surfers see is basically the same. Every ad is comprised of the following components:

- ➡ *Title*. A title can be up to 40 characters long. It should be brief, but attention getting.
- ➡ *Description*. This portion of your ad can only be 70 characters long. Again brevity is essential, but what you say must make an impact and appeal directly to your target audience. When possible, incorporate one or more of your keywords into the ad itself (in both the title and

the description). Two goals of your ad should be to announce that your online business offers the product the surfer is looking for and then to somehow differentiate your online business from the competition, which may also be advertising using ads that surround yours on the surfer's screen. One way to do this is to announce that you offer free shipping, or some other incentive for the potential customer.

➡ *Display URL.* This is the website address that is displayed within the ad. The actual link, however, can lead to a different website or a subpage within your domain. Ideally, the link should take surfers directly to the product description page for what they want, not your website's homepage. Don't make visitors who are responding to an ad have to search for the product they want. When clicked, the link in your ad should take them to that information.

From your perspective as the advertiser, it's easy to create and use a handful of ads that incorporate different headlines, keywords, and messages, and appeal to slightly different target audiences but lead to the same place—your website. In fact, it's common for online businesspeople to run several different campaigns simultaneously.

As you create your ads and each overall campaign, you need to build a list of relevant keywords that perfectly describe your product and/or your company. Who sees an ad depends heavily on the keywords associated with that ad. Ideally, your keywords should also correspond very closely to the content on your site. Each keyword can be a single word or a phrase that's up to 100 characters long. The web surfers who see your ad, of course, don't actually see this keyword list.

The service you use will help you select appropriate keywords if you're having trouble compiling your list. Most of the services allow advertisers to associate up to 50 unique keywords or phrases with each of their ads. As you create your keyword list, you do not have to use multiple variations of a single word (such as "widget" and "widgets"). Just make sure each word is spelled correctly.

Setting Your Budget

One of the best things about search engine marketing campaigns is that they can be created and launched with a very low budget. At least initially, you'll

---

CLICK TIP

Services like Yahoo! Search Engine Marketing, Google AdWords, and Microsoft AdCenter all offer in-depth tutorials for new advertisers using their services. You'll also find a selection of online tools to help you generate and monitor your ad campaigns. Make full use of these free services and tutorials to help you get the most out of every dollar spent on advertising. Ultimately, this helps you increase your profits.

---

probably want to experiment with a few different ad variations and keyword lists until you create an ad that has a low cost-per-click and high click-through rate. Once you've formulated one or more ads that generate appealing results, you should begin investing hundreds or thousands of dollars in that a campaign. Spending thousands on a campaign that generates poor results wastes your money and doesn't help you get the traffic that you want and need.

Online Display Advertising

Online display advertising allows you to purchase ad space on other websites that might appeal to your target audience. Your ads can have text, graphics, animation, sound, and even video to convey your marketing message. Unlike traditional print ads, however, someone who sees your online display ad can simply click on the ad, be transferred to your website in seconds, and gather more information or make a purchase.

Running online display ads on popular websites costs significantly more than using short, text-based search engine marketing ads. What your ad says and the visual elements used to convey the message are equally important. Thus, in addition to spending more to display your ads, you'll probably want to hire an advertising agency or graphic artist to design the ads to ensure they look professional and are appealing.

Depending on where you want your online display ads to appear, the size requirements, and ad content specifications, how much you pay will vary dramatically. In addition to choosing appropriate websites to advertise on, you need to select the exact placement of your ad on each website's page. Online

CLICK TIP

For many startup online businesses, using search engine marketing ads, as opposed to more costly online display advertising, is a more cost-effective and efficient way to initially generate traffic to a website.

real estate has value based on the number of people who might be seeing your ad and the physical size of your display ad, which is measured in pixels.

In general, the more people who might see your ad, the higher the ad rates. Depending on the website, however, you may have to pay based on overall impressions (the number of people who simply see your ad) or a pre-determined fee when people click on your ad. Another alternative is to pay a commission when a website offers a referral that results in a sale. The payment terms are typically created by the website on which you'll be advertising.

As the advertiser, your main objective after creating your display ad is to find the perfect websites to advertise on. These should be sites that directly appeal to your target audience. Ideally, you want your ad to be seen at precisely the moment someone wants to purchase the product you're offering.

The best way to find these websites is to put yourself in your target customer's shoes and begin surfing the web in search of sites that offer content that's appealing. Next, determine if those sites accept display advertising, and then request advertising information. Sites that accept display ads typically have a link on their homepage that says Advertise Here or Advertising Information.

Creating, launching, and managing a successful online display ad campaign requires specific skills. Instead of throwing away money on misguided advertising experiments, consider hiring an experienced advertising agency to help you if online display advertising is going to be part of your overall advertising, marketing, public relations, and promotional efforts for your business. You'll pay a bit more initially, but having the experience and expertise of an advertising professional generates much better results and higher sales.

Developing an Affiliate Program

One less expensive way to use online display advertising, and one that typically requires little or no initial out-of-pocket expense, is to set up an affiliate program. This requires recruiting other websites that cater to the same target audience as you to display your ad on their sites in exchange for a commission when a surfer clicks on your ad or buys something from your site as a result of a referral.

While LinkShare (888-742-7389, linkshare.com) continues to be the industry leader when it comes to administering an affiliate program, the following are just a few other

CLICK TIP

One way to generate added revenue from your website is to become an affiliate for other companies and display their ads on your site. If you sprinkle ads from well-established and well-known companies on your site, it can also boost your credibility among visitors.

companies that can help you run a successful affiliate program designed to build awareness of your business and generate traffic to your website:

- *Associate Programs*—associateprograms.com
- *Click Booth*—clickbooth.com
- *Commission Junction*—http://cju.cj.com
- *Commission Soup*—commissionsoup.com

There are also many other independent, third-party affiliate program agencies that can help you create and manage your program. Using any search engine, enter the search phrase "Affiliate Marketing" or "Affiliate Program."

CLICK TIP

AssociatePrograms.com offers a free tutorial on creating and managing an effective affiliate program. Point your browser to: associateprograms.com/articles/188/1/Affiliate-Program-Tutorial. Additional information can be found at http://onlinebusiness.about.com/od/affiliateprograms/a/affiliate.htm.

Price Comparison Websites: Drive Price-Conscious Consumers to Your Site

Savvy internet shoppers know they never have to pay full price for anything. If they want to find the absolute lowest price possible on virtually any item, they visit a price comparison website, enter in the exact name of the product they're looking for, and within seconds a listing of online merchants offering that product is displayed, along with their lowest advertised price for that product.

For your online business, advertising using a price comparison website (so you can be included in a list of referrals requested by a web surfer) can generate traffic to your site. The drawback, however, is that the potential customer is looking for the lowest price possible, and if you're not offering it, they simply shop elsewhere. If the product you're selling has a high profit margin or you're willing to compete with countless other online merchants mainly on price, price comparison websites can be an extremely viable sales tool.

This type of service also benefits merchants that focus on providing top-notch customer service, because the majority of these websites display customer ratings or rankings. A savvy web surfer/shopper knows to visit an online merchant that has both a lowest price and a high customer feedback, all of which is displayed on the price comparison website.

Some of the popular price comparison websites are:

➡ *AOL Shopping*—http://shopping.aol.com
➡ *BizRate*—bizrate.com
➡ *Nextag*—nextag.com, http://merchants.nextag.com/serv/main/ advertise/Advertise.do
➡ *Price Grabber*—pricegrabber.com/sell_here.php
➡ *Shopping.com*—shopping.com
➡ *Shopzilla*—shopzilla.com

Final Thoughts about Advertising Your Online Business

Based on the information in this chapter as well as the previous one, you've discovered that there are many different opportunities in the real world and in cyberspace that you can use to advertise, market, and promote your business. Depending on what you're selling, the target audience you're trying to reach, your level of creativity, your time frame, the resources you have available, and your budget, you'll want to pinpoint what combination of these opportunities will work best to drive traffic to your site so you can sell your product and generate profits.

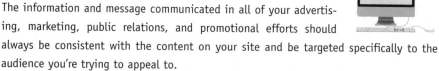

CLICK TIP

The information and message communicated in all of your advertising, marketing, public relations, and promotional efforts should always be consistent with the content on your site and be targeted specifically to the audience you're trying to appeal to.

Before investing vast amounts of money on any campaign, do your research, make projections, forecast response rates and potential profits, and whenever possible, test each element of your campaign before doing a full-scale launch. As you'll discover, many considerations and decisions go into media campaigns. The more time you invest developing your skills in these areas, doing your research, and analyzing your results, the better off you'll be.

Just remember, if you're not skilled or experienced in advertising, marketing, promotions, or public relations, you should consider hiring freelance experts or outside agencies to assist you, at least initially. It would help your business get off to a profitable start. Also, never put all of your eggs in a single basket. In this case, spread your advertising and marketing dollars around a bit and use a multifaceted approach to driving traffic to your website.

Finally, remember that no matter how successful your campaigns actually are, driving traffic to your website isn't enough. Once potential customers visit your site for the first time, the site's design, content, and ease of use must be appealing or they'll simply click the Back button on their browser and visit another online merchant to purchase whatever it is they're looking for.

What's Next

As you've probably discovered by now, operating a online business will require you to simultaneously juggle a handful of responsibilities, all of which are equally important to your business's success. The next chapter explains some of the ongoing business operations you'll need to handle, from order processing to order fulfillment (actually shipping product to your customers). The next chapter also discusses how to properly manage your inventory and the absolute importance of offering top-notch customer service to all of your customers.

Chapter 11

Managing Order Fulfillment and Everyday Business Operations

*C*ongratulations, you've found a product to sell, identified your target audience, launched your online business, and have begun marketing your business to drive traffic to your site. If all goes as planned, you should begin generating sales. At the same time, you'll be developing an ever-growing base of loyal customers.

As sales start to trickle in and you begin attracting potential new customers through your advertising and marketing efforts, it'll be necessary to fulfill orders, handle customer service issues, manage the bookkeeping tasks associated with running a business, maintain inventory, and take care of the many other responsibilities relating to operating a business.

While it's essential to develop well-thought-out strategies for handling every responsibility and task associated with your business's operation, at this point, what your new customers are most concerned about is receiving top-notch customer service and receiving their correctly fulfilled orders in a very timely manner.

Fulfilling Your Orders

As soon as someone places an order, he'll be expecting it to be fulfilled and shipped quickly, especially if he's opted to pay for rush shipping. To accommodate the demands of your customers, you need to establish order fulfillment procedures and a "shipping department" that maintains all of the inventory and shipping supplies needed to get all new orders quickly processed and shipped out.

For each product you're selling, you'll need to maintain an ample supply of appropriately sized boxes, padded envelopes, stuffing, packing tape, labels, and other shipping materials. Figure out exactly what you'll need and have a constant supply on hand.

Depending on the shipping options you've decided to extend to your customers, you'll need to develop relationships with the United States Postal Service (USPS), UPS, FedEx, DHL, and/or other shipping services in order to provide some or all of the following shipping options:

- Economy (five to seven days)
- 3-day
- 2nd-day
- Overnight

As an incentive to customers, some online business operators offer free economy (UPS/FedEx/DHL) or Priority Mail shipping (via the post office) and build these costs into the price of the product. Otherwise, your website's shopping cart module will need to calculate shipping charges and add them to the customer's total.

If you opt to ship your products via Priority Mail or Express Mail from the USPS, free envelopes and boxes are available. Based on the size of your product,

CLICK TIP

Having a postage machine in-house reduces to your local post office and saves you time waiting in line to purchase postage and drop off your packages.

you may also qualify for a flat shipping rate. For details about postage rates and to order free shipping supplies from the USPS, visit usps.com or your local post office branch.

To avoid daily trips to the local post office to buy stamps/postage and drop off packages, you can arrange for daily pick-up with your mail carrier but each package will need to have the proper postage already affixed. Thus, you might opt to acquire or rent a postage meter from a company like Pitney Bowes (pitneybowes.com). Several models are available, based on the amount of shipping you'll be doing.

For a startup business looking to generate postage stamps in-house for shipping, Endicia offers complete, low-cost postage solutions that allow any computer connected to the internet to purchase and print postage using any type of printer, including DYMO label printers (sold separately, starting under $200 at dymostamps.com). Endicia postage solutions are available for PC or Mac computers. Although the required software is free of charge and can be downloaded from the company's website (endicia.com), there is a monthly fee of $15.95 to maintain an account, plus the cost of whatever U.S. postage you purchase.

Depending on the shipping options you plan to offer to your customers, you'll probably need to open shipping accounts with FedEx, UPS, and/or DHL (and perhaps other couriers as well). Opening accounts with these companies takes just minutes and can be done online by visiting their websites. You can also order free shipping supplies (envelopes, labels, and boxes) from each company's website. They will be delivered right to your door. When opening an account, you'll typically need a major credit card.

To open an account with FedEx, UPS, and/or DHL, visit these websites:

➡ *FedEx*—FedEx.com
➡ *UPS*—UPS.com
➡ *DHL*—DHL.com

CLICK TIP

To quickly compare shipping rates among the couriers, visit iship.com/priceit/price.asp, redroller.com/shippingcenter/home, or http://pakmail.com/estimator.

CLICK TIP

No matter what you're shipping, it's a good idea to use a service that requires the recipient to sign for the package upon receipt. This may cost you a bit extra in shipping charges, but it can eliminate any confusion when a customer doesn't receive his order in a timely manner. Depending on what you're shipping, you may also need to purchase insurance for each package (at an additional cost) and/or use some of the other shipping services offered by the USPS, FedEx, UPS, DHL, and other couriers. You'll need to budget in all these shipping-related charges, including the cost of items like packing tape, stuffing, and labels, and pass these costs along to your customer by building them into the price of the product you're selling.

The prices these companies charge to ship your packages are based on several criteria, including the quantity of packages you ship on an ongoing basis (volume discounts apply), the shipping services you use, the size and weight of each package, your geographic location, and the destination of each package. To save money, you'll want to compare rates among these popular couriers. In many situations, the prices quoted to ship an identical package may be vastly different. You can also save money by dropping off your packages at a FedEx, USP, or DHL location rather than scheduling a pick-up.

As you pack up orders and prepare them for shipping, make sure you include ample padding or stuffing to ensure your product arrives at its destination undamaged. When developing the shipping policies and procedures for your company, you'll also need to determine what will be included in the packaging with each order. Some of your options include:

- A printed invoice
- A customer feedback card
- A printed catalog
- A personalized "Thank You for Your Order" letter
- Printed directions for returning or exchanging the product
- Special money-saving offers for repeat customers

From a record-keeping standpoint, you'll need to keep detailed records of your customers and related shipping and order details. Depending on the e-commerce turnkey solution you choose, these tools may be provided.

Otherwise, you'll need to acquire third-party software, such as ACT! (act.com), QuickBooks (insuit.com), or FileMaker Pro (filemaker.com) to help you manage these important tasks.

It's essential that you be able to quickly track any orders you've shipped, so having the applicable customer and shipping information at your disposal is important. You also need contingency plans in place to deal with a wide range of potential scenarios and problems, including:

- An order arrives to its destination damaged.
- An order gets delayed being shipped out.
- An order gets lost in transit.
- The customer wishes to cancel or change her order before it gets processed.
- The customer wants to return the product.
- The customer wants to exchange her order.
- The order was incorrectly fulfilled.

Dealing with these and other issues, which will no doubt arise, requires you to interact directly with your customers as well as with the shipping company you used. Remember, regardless of the situation, always strive to provide prompt, courteous, and highly professional customer service. Your goal should be to quickly transform any potentially negative situation into a positive one (from your customer's perspective) in order to retain him as a valued customer, generate repeat business, and increase your chances of benefitting from positive word-of-mouth advertising.

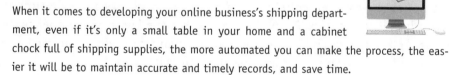

CLICK TIP

When it comes to developing your online business's shipping department, even if it's only a small table in your home and a cabinet chock full of shipping supplies, the more automated you can make the process, the easier it will be to maintain accurate and timely records, and save time.

Managing Your Inventory

Depending on what you're selling, from whom you're buying (wholesalers, distributors, importers, manufacturers, etc.), or from where you're acquiring your manufacturing materials, one of the challenges of an online business is ensuring you always have ample inventory on hand to fulfill your customers' demands. Being sold out of a product or having to delay fulfilling an order by more than a few days could easily result in an unhappy customer and a lost sale.

Having too much inventory on hand requires an additional financial investment, warehousing space, and additional insurance. If you're maintaining any inventory in your home, office, or an outside warehouse/storage facility, you'll need to have insurance to protect this investment. Your homeowner's insurance will probably not cover business-related inventory or equipment against theft, damage, or other mishaps.

Providing Top-Notch Customer Service

No matter what you're selling or to whom you're selling, all potential or actual customers you interact with online, over the telephone, through the mail, or in-person must always feel as if they're your most important customer. Their satisfaction and happiness is the key to your success, and every aspect of how you do business should somehow take into account what makes your customers happy.

Satisfied customers often become repeat customers. From an expense standpoint as a business operator, it's always less costly to generate repeat business from an existing customer than it is to find a new customer and make a sale. In addition, satisfied customers provide positive feedback and testimonials you can use, and they're more apt to provide positive word-of-mouth advertising on your behalf (another very inexpensive way to generate new business).

On the flip side, dissatisfied customers require more of your valuable time to fix or remedy the situation. They could easily generate negative word-of-mouth publicity for your company, which could quickly become detrimental and result in lost business. People who are dissatisfied with an experience they have dealing with a merchant are apt to complain to their credit card company, friends, co-workers, and anyone else who will listen.

Just as your products should address your customers' needs and wants; potentially help them save time or money; and/or somehow make their life more enjoyable, pleasurable, less stressful, or easier, the same should hold true for every interaction you have with each of your customers, This includes their experience exploring your website, placing their order, having their questions and concerns answered, or having any problems they may encounter with the product you're selling.

In addition to conveying a professional and friendly attitude, some of the things you can do automatically to improve each customer's experience dealing with your company include

➡ Sending an autoresponse "Thank You for Your Order" e-mail as soon as a new order is received.

➡ Sending a follow-up e-mail when an order ships, with tracking information and anticipated date of arrival.

➡ Offering a special discount or moneysaving offer to repeat customers.

➡ Offering an incentive for current customers to provide you with referrals.

➡ Encouraging customers to interact with you online via e-mail, online, or chat, or by telephone.

➡ Shipping all orders promptly.

➡ Responding to all inquiries, problems, return requests, etc., within 24 hours of receiving them—sooner, if possible.

Offering the best customer service experience possible to your customers does not have to cost a fortune. It's all about maintaining the right attitude and conveying that attitude in every aspect of your business, from the direct interaction with your customers to the text displayed on your website. In fact, if done correctly, offering top-notch customer service should cost next to nothing. The long-term benefits to your business, however, are incalculable.

Growing Your Business

Operating any business, as you already know, requires a detailed business plan to help you get started. Part of this plan should include a strategy for growing and expanding your business over time. Ask yourself where you'd like your business to be in 3, 6, and 12 months, as well as in 1, 3, and 5 years. Then, determine what it takes to achieve those objectives and start implementing those efforts accordingly.

As your business grows and you generate more and more orders, you may want to expand the functionality of your website, add new features, and/or start selling additional products. To generate additional repeat business, you also want to find creative ways to continuously update the content on your site and give people reasons to return to your site often. Maintaining a blog or newsletter that's updated weekly, for example, gives people a reason to revisit your site (as long as the content of your newsletter or blog is interesting and seen as valuable to your readers).

Transforming a startup online business into a profitable one takes considerable time and dedication. Once this happens, however, you want take steps to grow the business. Thus, you may also need to consider hiring employees, finding office space (instead of working from your home), and/or quitting your current job to operate your business full time.

To successfully transform a startup business into a profitable one also takes persistence and patience. Try to anticipate problems or obstacles you might run into, and develop plans in advance for dealing with them quickly and efficiently. If you're prepared when you hit a snag, it'll take you less time and cost less money to recover, allowing you to focus your time and efforts on more productive endeavors. Being prepared and having contingency plans in place also reduces your stress and ensures you're able to promptly and effectively deal with whatever arises.

Be sure to maintain realistic expectations for your business and its growth potential, stay on top of all of your responsibilities as a business operator (including those tasks you don't find enjoyable), and always keep up-to-date on the latest trends and technological developments in e-commerce. As your e-commerce turnkey solution offers new features and functionality, determine whether it's beneficial to incorporate these new developments, tools, or business practices into your site.

At the same time, keep up with all of the latest trends and developments in the industry that your product relates to, so you can address the ever-changing demands and needs of your customers.

Finally, keep close tabs on your competition. Keep track of what they're doing and take steps to do it better—whether it's providing superior customer service, lower prices, higher quality products, more attractive customer incentives, a more professional-looking website, or a more efficient shopping cart module. Try to learn from your competition's mistakes, while at the same time, try to benefit from their research, business practices, and policies, and their overall business model.

Keep Track of Your Startup

Throughout this book, you've learned about the major steps necessary to launch a successful online business, and you've discovered how to master many of the skills that are necessary to operate your business effectively and profitably. To help you recap and plan your schedule as you get your business up and running, use Figure 11.1: Online Business Startup Checklist.

Not all of these steps are necessary. They depend on the type of business you plan to launch and what you will ultimately be selling. In addition, the order in which you complete these key steps may vary.

Figure 11.1: **ONLINE BUSINESS STARTUP CHECKLIST**

To Do	Completed	Task Description	Notes
❏	❏	Develop a list of potential products to sell, and research them.	
❏	❏	Determine your target customer base.	
❏	❏	Create a detailed business plan (in writing).	
❏	❏	Brainstorm a name for your business.	
❏	❏	Obtain the computer equipment, internet access, software, and business equipment and supplies you need to get started.	
❏	❏	Register your business with your local and state government and the IRS. (This step might include incorporating your business or setting up a DBA.)	
❏	❏	Establish the infrastructure of your business, including your bookkeeping practices.	
❏	❏	Based on your financial projections and the information detailed in your business plan, develop a realistic budget and raise the startup money needed to launch your business.	

Figure 11.1: **ONLINE BUSINESS STARTUP CHECKLIST,** CONTINUED

To Do	Completed	Task Description	Notes
❏	❏	Register one or more domain names (.com).	
❏	❏	Research e-commerce turnkey solutions and find one that meets your needs and start using it.	
❏	❏	Research sources for acquiring the product you wish to sell, including distributors, manufacturers, wholesalers, importers, etc.	
❏	❏	Create detailed product descriptions and acquire professional-quality photos of the products you plan to sell.	
❏	❏	Gather all of the content and additional assets you'll incorporate into your website.	
❏	❏	Create a company logo and the other graphic assets you plan to incorporate into your website.	
❏	❏	Develop a strategy to process online payments, such as obtaining a merchant account and/or registering as a merchant with PayPal and/or Google Checkout.	
❏	❏	Develop and launch a detailed, multifaceted marketing, advertising, promotional, and public relations campaign.	
❏	❏	Acquire an ample supply of product inventory to get started, and develop business relationships with your key suppliers.	

Figure 11.1: **ONLINE BUSINESS STARTUP CHECKLIST,** CONTINUED

To Do	Completed	Task Description	Notes
❑	❑	Hire freelancers to help you plan, develop, launch, and maintain your website, and operate your business.	
❑	❑	Analyze your potential competition.	
❑	❑	Create your website and add all of the functionality you'll need to effectively sell your product. Focus on creating a professional, well-designed, and easy-to-navigate site.	
❑	❑	Before launching your website, test it carefully and ensure it contains no dead links, typographical errors, or other problems.	
❑	❑	Hire website testers and have them thoroughly test your entire website looking for typos, dead links, and other problems.	
❑	❑	Establish your business's policies and operational procedures, including how you'll approach customer service.	
❑	❑	Create your company's shipping department and develop detailed procedures for promptly and accurately fulfilling orders.	
❑	❑	Focus on getting your site listed with the search engines and then on search engine optimization.	

Figure 11.1: **ONLINE BUSINESS STARTUP CHECKLIST,** CONTINUED

To Do	Completed	Task Description	Notes
❑	❑	Carefully monitor all aspects of your business and fine-tune your operational procedures and practices as necessary.	
❑	❑	Track the success of all marketing, advertising, and promotional efforts, and fine-tune your strategies to generate the most traffic to your site possible, while incurring the lowest possible expense.	
❑	❑	Start planning how you'll expand your online business in the future.	

Chapter 12

Learn from Other E-Commerce Business Operators

*I*t's one thing to read about the steps involved with starting an online business and the core skills you'll need to be successful. It's another thing altogether to have the chance to speak one-on-one with already successful online business owners and learn firsthand from their real-world experience.

If you have the chance to sit down face-to-face with people who are currently running online businesses, you can learn a lot from their success, experience, and past mistakes. You are strongly urged to take advantage of such an opportunity. To help you get started, this chapter features in-depth interviews with six online businesspeople who share their knowledge and insight. The information and tips you'll read in this section come directly from people who have firsthand experience launching and operating an e-commerce website.

Eric Mindel
Co-Founder, Positive Development, LCC
Website: www.PeppyParents.com

In 2006, Eric Mindel and his wife Heather both held full-time jobs. However, when their second child was born, as parents they believed it was important for at least one of them to stay home to raise their kids. Instead of giving up one of their incomes, the couple opted to launch an online business, called PeppyParents.com, from their home.

By tapping their experience as parents as well as their professional experience, Eric and Heather were able to define a need for specific types of high-end childcare and parenting products. After spending almost six months planning their business and developing a detailed business plan, PeppyParents.com was launched using the eBay ProStores e-commerce turnkey solution.

In this interview, company founder Eric Mindel shares his experiences with creating, launching, and now maintaining what has become a successful online business. Thanks to plenty of planning and a well-defined business plan, Mindel reported that his business broke even several months ahead of schedule and has since dramatically surpassed sales projections.

What made you want to start an online business?

Mindel: "We had been talking about starting an online business, on a part-time basis, for a while. When our second child was born, we decided it was time to make it happen. My professional background involves working on the internet, so we were able to skip some of the initial learning curve involved."

Where did the idea for your business come from?

Mindel: "We wanted to run a business based on something we were truly passionate and knowledgeable about. We pinpointed an opportunity to introduce parents, like ourselves, to products that are not readily available from baby superstores. We knew about many upscale products that catered to many different lifestyles, and we felt we could help parents by offering products that provided valuable solutions to many different types of parenting needs. We also wanted to find a business opportunity that would be resistant to economic dips. People are always having babies, so we developed our idea for PeppyParents.com."

After coming up with the idea, how did the business come together?

Mindel: "A lot of my professional background is in web technologies, so I have been working for various dotcom businesses since 1995. E-commerce was second nature to me. Instead of having to invest a lot of time learning how to sell products online, we focused our energies on creating a detailed business, financial, and marketing plan. I am not a programmer, so I wanted to find a turnkey e-commerce solution that could get us off the ground running, without having to make a huge investment in programming.

"Initially, when we launched PeppyParents.com, we sold about 60 different products, divided into several high-end categories, all of interest to parents of infants and young children. We began with tens of thousands of dollars in startup capital, which came from our savings. Much of this money was invested in purchasing our initial inventory. Early on, based on our research and our goal of offering the best customer service possible, we decided against having our suppliers drop ship products to our customers. This meant we needed to build up and maintain an inventory of each product. For us, drop-shipping simply wasn't an option if we wanted to provide the level of customer service we knew was important. We wanted control over our order fulfillment and shipping, without having to rely on drop shippers."

What made you decide to use eBay ProStores?

Mindel: "I did extensive research about many of the turkey solutions that were out there. The tools offered by GoDaddy.com, for example, didn't seem robust or flexible enough to meet our needs. I also looked at Yahoo! Stores. However, our initial plan was to also utilize eBay auctions to sell some of our products as we built up our customer base. eBay ProStores seemed to work more seamlessly with eBay auctions, which was in line with what we were trying to accomplish.

"Also, I liked the easy integration between PayPal and ProStores. My goal was to get up and running with a fully functional website as quickly as possible. I also wanted complete flexibility to expand and modify our website in the future. When I looked at Yahoo! Stores versus ProStores, for me, ProStores offered the most options for flexibility in terms of offering Google Checkout and PayPal as online payment options, for example. I was also looking for a solution that would last us for at least several years."

How much time was required prior to launching your business?

Mindel: "Prior to launching the site, we invested about six months, working part time, on the business plan and overall planning process. A lot of that time was spent learning the ropes and learning how to negotiate with suppliers and manufacturers. We spent a lot of time figuring out budgets and making sales projections. I also did a lot of customization to our ProStores template prior to launch. I estimate I invested between 200 to 300 hours in that process alone. If I had just wanted to grab one of their templates and add my product details and artwork, I could have been up and running in 30 hours. I wanted something, however, that was cleaner, more professional, and more customized looking."

What is a typical workday/week like for you?

Mindel: "Currently, I still hold down a full-time job and my wife is raising our kids from home, but we both also work part time on this project. I work on PeppyParents.com at night and on weekends. Between the two of us, we spend about eight to ten hours per day running the online business. The day-to-day operation of our business is done from our home office. However, we maintain an outside storage facility where we keep our inventory.

"During the day, my wife handles the customer service and bookkeeping, using QuickBooks. After work, I drop by our warehouse, fulfill the day's orders, and do a package drop off at our local FedEx location. I'm typically home in time for dinner."

What was the biggest misconception you had about e-commerce?

Mindel: "I don't know that I had any misconceptions. Nothing has caught us by surprise, and I attribute this to really good planning and my previous experience doing stuff on the internet since 1995, developing web applications for research purposes.

"I think a common misconception that other people have is that if you build an awesome website, you'll automatically generate a lot of visitors to it. Maintaining this philosophy can lead to a serious downfall. A mediocre website with an excellent marketing plan will do infinitely better than an awesome website with a mediocre or no marketing plan.

"To initially generate traffic to the site when we launched, we sent out a massive e-mail to all of our friends and family announcing the business and asking for their word-of-mouth referral support. We also got involved in several online advertising opportunities with Yahoo!, Shopzilla, PriceGrabber, and Google AdWords. I put a lot of effort into search engine optimization, which is a time-consuming and ongoing process. Instead of doing SEO for just the online business, I do it for our individual products as well, to ensure potential customers can easily find us on the search engines if they do product or category-specific searches, as opposed to a search for our particular company. My effort has been to really study what works in terms of our marketing and advertising, and to constantly fine-tune those efforts.

"I believe one reason why we've been successful is because we've blasted our marketing efforts among many different channels over the past year. We've discovered that while one of our products may do phenomenally well using one marketing channel, it might not do anywhere near as well using another channel. This has involved a learning curve in order to get the most marketing bang out of our advertising dollars.

"In terms of the SEO work, I do this myself. But, if I didn't come into this business with the professional background that I had, there would be no way I could do it."

As you got your business up and running, what were some of the challenges or pitfalls you faced?

Mindel: "We haven't really encountered any serious problems, mainly because of our planning. We always made projections and financial forecasts, for example, based on the worst-case scenario. This helped to ensure that our cash flow would be stable. This past December, we experienced five times the sales we had projected. This kind of growth is awesome, but at the same time, it has forced us to get up to speed on inventory management. With too much inventory on hand, you tie up your capital. With too little inventory on hand, you lose sales. Proper inventory management has been a skill we needed to learn. Having far better than anticipated sales, however, is an amazing problem to have.

"One thing we didn't anticipate when we first got started was that many of our distributors and premium product suppliers have pricing agreements in place. This means that we can't offer discounts on many of the items we sell. This prevented us from being able to use eBay auctions initially to help launch our business. On the positive side, it also helped to ensure that our competition could not undercut us from a pricing standpoint."

As you were developing your website, what did you do to gather all of your product photography and artwork?

Mindel: "A lot of the manufacturers we opted to work with provided high-quality product images upon request. I also have all of the equipment we need to do our own professional-quality product shots in-house. One of my hobbies has always been photography, so even before launching this business, I had professional, studio-quality photography equipment in my home. I just hadn't ever photographed items like pacifiers or baby blankets, until we launched this business."

Do you have any other advice for someone getting started in launching their own online business?

Mindel: "I think proper planning before you launch your business is essential. Learn how to create a detailed business plan and do it. When you get started, you already need to have a clear understanding of what your expenses are going to be. This will help you determine, in advance, if your business idea is even feasible. Before you launch your business, you need to know how much money you're going to need. My advice is to assume the worst-case scenario as you plan your cash flow needs.

"When designing your actual website, having good usability standards is imperative. Also, having good navigation within your site is important. Regardless of what you're selling, you'll probably have to deal with multiple competitors. When someone first visits your site, you've got just six to eight seconds to capture their attention, or they're going to leave.

"In terms of search engine optimization, learn as much about this topic as you can, even if you plan to hire an outside specialist or third-party company to handle this for you. You don't have to be a techie to understand the basic principles involved with effective search engine optimization, which is essential for any online business. For example, you should understand how to use meta tags, and know that it's important to include plenty of keywords within the text-based content of your site, as opposed to within graphic elements.

"Plenty of people call themselves SEO professionals. Some of these people know what they're doing. Others might not. By having a basic understanding of what's possible and what needs to get done, you'll be in a better position to make sure it's done correctly, without overpaying for this service."

Have you seen any positive or negative trends in the e-commerce industry as a whole?

Mindel: "One e-commerce-related topic I've been watching closely is what will happen with the sales tax laws. Right now, one incentive for people to shop online is so they don't have to pay sales tax on many types of purchases. If laws change, this could negatively impact some online business operators. For customers who are not in an extreme rush to receive their products, ordering them online and not having to pay sales tax is a definite incentive over shopping at a local retail store.

"I am also looking closely at technological advancements happening with mobile phones and wireless handheld devices that are capable of surfing the web. This technology is changing rapidly and could provide tremendous e-commerce opportunities in the not-so-distance future."

Brian Seed
Co-Founder, *Organic Sleep Products*
Website: www.organicsleepproducts.com

In September 2005, Brian Seed founded a retail store and manufacturing facility in Bend, Oregon, called Organic Sleep Products. The business continues to specialize in selling only certified organic, green, and all-natural bedding products: including mattress sets, mattress toppers, pillows, sheets, blankets, duvet covers, and related products. He launched this retail store after pursuing a successful career as a music teacher, a profession he had to abandon when he started suffering from rheumatoid arthritis.

In 2006, Seed decided it was time to expand his business by launching an e-commerce website so he could more easily make his unique collection of quality bedding products available to people throughout the world. In this interview, Seed discusses his experience launching and managing the online aspect of his business.

What made you want to add an online component to your business?

Seed: "About 85 percent of the country does not have a local retailer for the all-natural bedding products that Organic Sleep Products offers, so launching an e-commerce site was pretty much a necessity if I wanted to expand the business. We offer completely organic and all-natural bed and bedding solutions that use absolutely no synthetics or chemicals."

After you decided to create an e-commerce website, how did the process unfold?

Seed: "After I decided this was the direction I wanted to go with the business, I needed to find a turnkey solution that was capable of meeting our needs. Organic Sleep Products already had its own merchant account through our local bank, and we used Authorize.net as our gateway to process our credit card transactions. One of the challenges I faced initially was finding an e-commerce turnkey solution that was compatible with my existing merchant account. For me, this was the piece of the puzzle that took the longest to figure out.

"Prior to launching OrganicSleepProducts.com, we had operated informational websites, but none that had e-commerce functionality. I selected to use Yahoo! Stores because I liked the overall platform. It was easy to create our online catalog of products, plus I liked the way Yahoo! Stores made it quick and easy to process an order that would require USPS shipping. To get the site online, I did everything myself, using the site design tools provided by Yahoo! Stores. Initially, I created the product descriptions and then used photographs provided by my product vendors. It was time consuming putting the online catalog together, but it was not a technical process.

"From the point I decided to create an e-commerce website to the time it actually went online and was open for business, the process took about two to three weeks, but I was working on the project off and on when I didn't have customers in the retail store.

"In terms of the financial investment required to bring the business online, our investment was reasonably small in the scheme of things. Based on the return we've had after 14 months of being online, the initial expense has been well worth the investment."

Now that the site is fully operational, how much time do you spend maintaining it?

Seed: "Only about 15 minutes per day. When an order comes in, it's handled in the same way as our retail orders, so the process of packing up and shipping items is fast and easy."

What was the biggest misconception you had when you first launched the dotcom aspect of your business?

Seed: "Like so many other new online business operators, I didn't realize how necessary it is to market and advertise the website in order to generate traffic to it. When you launch a site, it's like putting a sign up in the desert. You need to convince people to visit your site. Being a niche company, I didn't realize it would take time for the site to actually become established.

"Initially, we bought into Yahoo! Search Marketing pretty heavily. For people first attempting this, I strongly recommend that you set aside a budget for this and that you stick to that budget. You may notice that your competitors will boost your costs by clicking on your ads themselves or bidding more for a higher ranking themselves. I recommend that you approach search marketing from an advertising perspective, just as you would when launching a radio or print advertising campaign. Know how much you have to spend, and then spend those funds wisely.

"Our business has had better success using Google AdWords than Yahoo! Search Marketing. Now, I look very closely to where all of our visitors are coming from, and I adjust my search marketing budget and advertising dollars accordingly."

After launching your online business, did you encounter any initial pitfalls or problems?

Seed: "As an online merchant, you definitely want to be very cautious with your internet security and your acceptance of credit card payments. Set up your order processing system to flag potentially fraudulent orders or transactions. For example, verify that addresses and zip codes match up. Visa, MasterCard, American Express, and Discover will provide you, the merchant, with an authorization code, but when it comes to e-commerce, that code could be really meaningless.

"If a sale turns out to involve a fraudulent credit card transaction, you as the online merchant are 100 percent liable for it. They're going to take all of the money back from you, plus they won't reimburse you for your processing fees. If you shipped the product or had any other fees associated with the sale, you could lose more money than the actual sale. This is not the case with a traditional brick-and-mortar retail store when the credit card is present and you swipe it through the credit card processing machine in your store. If you swipe a physical credit card, the merchant is not responsible for any fraudulent transactions. This is a drawback for online merchants that isn't very well advertised."

Do you have any other tips for success as an online business operator?

Seed: "The more people you can get to put your website address on their website, through a referral program, link exchange, or inclusion in blogs, for example, the better off you'll be. Using public relations to generate positive reviews in the media for your product is also very helpful.

"Another thing online business operators should strive for is to offer the very best customer service possible. This is extremely important. Running an online business is not a total virtual environment. You may have to interact with your customers by telephone, mail, or even in person. Customers are going to call and e-mail you with questions, and you need to respond to them properly. As an online business operator, you need to build up customer loyalty, just as you would for any type of business. If people are treated well, you'll get repeat business and positive word-of-mouth advertising from them."

Is there anything else you think potential online business operators should know before they get started?

Seed: "The first year is going to be a struggle. It takes time to get your site noticed, and there is a learning curve involved with being an online business operator. To get everything right will take time. After you hit your 12-month anniversary, things tend to get easier from many different perspectives. For example, you'll receive better placement on the internet search engines you're already registered with, because these sites pay attention to how long you've been in business."

Nancy Kerrigan
Co-Founder, PetsAtPlay.com
Website: www.PetsAtPlay.com

Company founder Nancy Kerrigan (no, not the Olympic ice skater) has been a designer and inventor for more than 25 years. It wasn't until she adopted her Shih Tzu named Maggie, and designed several high-end products for her, including her patented Sleep-N-Store dog bed and the Harness Play Pack, that she founded Pets At Play.

Kerrigan spends most of her time designing and inventing new products. Several have been prominently featured on national and international television shows, as well as in national magazines. That led her to the conclusion that she needed to launch an e-commerce website to fulfill orders for her products, although the main thrust of her business is selling her inventions through wholesalers, distributors, and retailers.

Kerrigan is first to admit that she's not too internet savvy. This lack of knowledge caused her initially to spend far too much money to have her company's e-commerce website designed and programmed from scratch. Over the years, however, she's learned the ins and outs of e-commerce and how to sell her products using the web, becoming much more knowledgeable in these areas.

What made you start PetsAtPlay.com as an online business?

Kerrigan: "When I invented the Harness Play Pack for dogs, I wanted to create a place on the internet where people could go to view the product, learn more about it, and order it. The goal with my inventions is to sell primarily to wholesalers, distributors, and dealers; however, I also saw an opportunity to sell my inventions directly to consumers via the web. I thought having a website would help to legitimize my business.

"PetsAtPlay.com launched in 2003. At the time, my then business partner and I initially invested over $20,000 to have the website developed from scratch. When my partnership ended, however, I then needed to redesign the website at an additional cost of $6,000. At the time, the few e-commerce solutions that were available were not as robust or as powerful as they are today."

From the time you decided to launch an e-commerce site to the point where the business was launched, how long did it take?

Kerrigan: "It took almost eight months to get the initial site up and running. When the site needed to be redesigned, that took almost three additional months. Again, these were websites being created from scratch. I had to hire several programmers to accomplish what I needed."

Now that you have an e-commerce site that's fully operational, how much time do you spend in a typical day or week running the online aspect of your business?

Kerrigan: "I have hired someone to handle all of the website maintenance and operation. I am responsible for fulfilling the orders. How long it takes varies, because I don't do any paid advertising. All of the traffic to the site is a result of free publicity the company or my products receive, or it's generated through word-of-mouth among dog owners. I tend to receive orders in spurts, especially around the holidays.

"Being the inventor of the products I'm selling, my goal is to get retailers to sell my products in their stores. Many of these retailers would prefer that I don't sell my products directly to consumers on the web because they look at it as competition. Thus, the e-commerce aspect of my business is of secondary importance to me.

"Initially, when I launched the PetsAtPlay.com website, I did a bunch of advertising in special interest magazines for dog lovers and pet owners. The orders then came in based on when the new issues of those magazines were published. During the busiest times of the year, I'd only have to spend several hours per day fulfilling orders and handling customer service-related issues."

What would you say was the biggest misconception you had about launching and then running an online business?

Kerrigan: "The reality of how the whole process worked was very different from what I thought it would be. I originally had it in my head that as soon as I made my website available online, I'd become a millionaire selling my products to customers from all over the world. That hasn't happened yet, although the business is doing well."

What additional types of advertising and promotions did you do initially?

Kerrigan: "I never did any paid online advertising. Aside from the print ads in magazines, my focus has been on generating free publicity using grassroots public relations efforts. Over the years, my products have been featured on *The*

Tonight Show, CNN, HGTV, and dozens of other televisions shows. I've also appeared multiple times on the *Home Shopping Network* to promote and sell my various inventions and dog products. Just one appearance on *HGTV*, for example, sold more pet beds that I could have imagined.

"My Sleep-N-Store dog bed, for example, is unique. They're handmade, and designed to be a piece of luxury furniture in someone's home. Thus, my target audience for this product is upscale dog owners willing and able to spend hundreds of dollars for this type of ultra-luxurious product. If I didn't have a website, the people who saw this product, for example, on the various national television shows that I have appeared on, would not have been able to purchase it easily."

What are some of the important lessons you've learned about operating an online business?

Kerrigan: "It's extremely important to continuously update your website and add new content to it. This is something I don't do as often as I should, because the online component of my overall business is not my main objective. Plus, I don't have the expertise to make changes to the site myself.

"Before someone starts their online business, they should do plenty of research and really develop an understanding of what's involved from both a time and financial standpoint. I had to learn absolutely everything from the ground up, because I wasn't really prepared to launch this type of business initially. If you don't know what you're doing, make sure you find and hire someone who does, but also make sure you don't overpay for their services."

Michael Alahverdian
Professional Website Designer
Website: www.andrastos.com

Thus far, you've read a handful of interviews within this chapter with people who have successfully launched an online business venture. Prior to starting their business, most of these people had little or no computer programming or website design knowledge, and learned many of the necessary skills required as the need for each arose.

Michael Alahverdian, however, is a professional website designer for Wakefield, Rhode Island-based NetSense Internet Solutions (www.netsense.net).

He has more than six years worth of experience, plus extensive training in a variety of programming languages and website design tools.

Alahverdian currently works full-time for NetSense Internet Solutions, but also works as a freelance website designer during his off-time. He is responsible for actually designing and programming dozens of successful e-commerce websites and knows what it takes for a website to achieve success when it comes to attracting and retaining visitors and then converting them into paying customers.

In this interview, Alahverdian shares a different but extremely important perspective in terms of website design and maintenance. If you opt to use a complete e-commerce turnkey solution to design and operate your website, you may never need the services of an experienced and skilled website designer. However, if you decide to have your e-commerce website designed from scratch, or if you use the OSCommerce solution (see Chapter 6), you definitely want to use the skills of a freelance website designer to create and launch your site.

How did you get started in web design?

Alahverdian: "I got started about six years ago, working for a small, dial-up internet service company doing tech support. When the dial-up business slowed down, the company started doing web design work, so that's when I started programming websites professionally. I work with HTML and ColdFusion mostly, but I am proficient with a variety of programming languages and websites design tools. ColdFusion is a server technology used for rapid application development.

"I work full time doing web application development for NetSense, but I also do web application development in my off-hours by picking up freelance projects outside of work. I have worked with many startup e-commerce businesses and have helped them grow over time. What online business owners need to understand upfront is that once a site is programmed and fully operational, down the road, it will need to be maintained and updated on a regular basis. It's important to develop a long-term relationship with the programmer or website designer you hire."

When someone approaches you for a new website development project, what information do you need to know to get started and how does the process work?

Alahverdian: "I generally ask them why they want a website. A lot of people have serious misconceptions about how websites work and what they're capable of. My first goal is to help the potential client develop realistic expectations and a good understanding of what launching an e-commerce website entails.

"If you build a website, it's like placing a business card on the world's largest coffee table. Someone might stumble upon it by accident, but otherwise, nobody is going to know how to find your business card and call you. This is why marketing and advertising your website is essential in order to drive traffic to it. A website is something that needs to be properly promoted to your target audience, plus the content of the site must have a specific objective. For example, it can be a communications tool or an interactive brochure, or it can be a catalog through which you accept online orders.

"After determining the website's purpose, it must be designed in such a way that it's attractive, professional-looking, easy to use, and comfortable for visitors. If your website looks like it was created ten years ago, people will feel the same way about the products you're selling."

What information or content does an e-commerce business owner need to supply so you can start creating a website?

Alahverdian: "This will vary, depending on the goals of the website. At the very least, I will need your final, edited text that you want displayed anywhere on the website. Web designers are not the people you want writing your copy. That's not our specialty. Our job is to create a highly functional and easy-to-use website. You also want to supply any other content, such as product photographs, video clips in digital form, audio, or other multimedia assets that you want incorporated into your website.

"The need for having professional-quality photos showcased throughout an e-commerce website is essential. Another key asset you'll need to supply is your company's logo. This will allow the website designer to create your site's look based on the image and the color scheme of that logo.

"One thing I always suggest is that the business owner spend time surfing the web looking for websites they like. If they can show me five to ten websites that appeal to them—based on look, design, and functionality—this gives me tremendous insight into what the client wants for their own site and it saves a lot of guesswork. Look carefully at color schemes, layouts, and features when doing your surfing."

When someone is looking to hire a website designer, what should they look for?

Alahverdian: "First, focus on experience and credentials. Make sure the website designer has experience developing the type of website you're looking to have created. Second, look carefully at their portfolio of work and make sure you like what you see. Someone might have programming knowledge, but not the artistic or creative skills to design appealing and professional-looking websites.

"When you're looking at a designer's credentials, make sure he or she has the ability to create sites from scratch and not just plug your content into someone else's template. If a designer claims to be an expert using Dream-Weaver, this can be good or bad. Make sure that they also know how to program and code. Specially ask if the website designer is proficient using HTML.

"It's also essential that the website designer be able to work with all of the latest versions of the current development tools. Proficiency in FrontPage, for example, was impressive a few years ago, but this development tool is out-dated."

What should someone expect to pay to hire a professional and experienced website designer/programmer?

Alahverdian: "From the e-commerce business owner's standpoint, it's almost always cheaper and easier to negotiate a per-project rate with a website designer, as opposed to an hourly rate. Based on someone's knowledge and experience, the time it takes them to complete a task will vary greatly. It's better to define, in writing, exactly what you need and when you need it, and then negotiate a flat rate for that project. You can then negotiate a separate hourly rate for website updates, but make sure the designer is willing to charge you in quarter-hour increments, since many types of website changes or updates can be done very quickly by someone who knows what they're doing.

"When negotiating with a website designer, what's expected of them should be written out in detail, along with deadlines and other expectations. There should be no room for misunderstandings. If you want a website containing seven pages that will showcase 50 products, for example, and you need it completed in three weeks, this is what should be described in the contract, along with the flat rate you agree on.

"If you agree to an hourly rate and the website designer spends 15 hours, at $100 per hour, to design a website that you absolutely hate or that does not have the functionality you need, you'll then need to pay an additional $1,500 to have the site redone. If you agree to a flat rate, then you know how much it will cost to get the website you want created and there will be no surprises. Expect that once a website is created, you will want or need to make changes and fine-tune the site before it goes online.

"The hourly rate for an experienced website designer based in the United States will be anywhere from $50 to $150. If you hire someone who is competent, a basic e-commerce website can typically be created, using static content, within one or two days. I can usually create a site within eight hours, but I have friends who can do the same level of work, but it might take them two full days.

"When you look at a potential designer's portfolio, ask questions, such as 'How much did this website cost?' and 'How long did this take you to develop?' These questions will help you determine how quickly the designer is capable of working, help you calculate costs, plus offers a preview of the quality of their work. Don't just focus on someone's hourly rate. Determine how much that designer will be able to get done in a typical hour and look closely at the quality of their work."

To save money, should someone purchase a website template and then hire a website designer or programmer to simply customize that template to create a website?

Alahverdian: "The website template companies offer a great way to preview hundreds or even thousands of potential site designs quickly. The problem with templates is that hundreds of other companies can purchase that same template and then will have a very similar looking website to yours. Having a generic looking website, with a design that people have seen before, takes away from your company's uniqueness and credibility. On the web, you never want to look like a cookie-cutter business that threw together a generic-looking website. Having a unique design is extremely important, and it's not too expensive. A good designer should be able to create a totally original website design for you, for less than $1,000 to $1,500."

Should a formal contract be created between the business operator and a website designer?

Alahverdian: "You should definitely create a written document that spells everything out and that's signed by both parties. The document should describe the work to be done and when it needs to be completed by. It should also state how updates and changes, or how fine-tuning to the site will be handled. This document does not have to be created by a lawyer, but it should be signed and dated by both parties and be considered a formal business agreement. The more detail that's in the contract, in regard to what's expected and what's desired, the better off you'll be."

Should an online business owner consider outsourcing their website design work to programmers in another country?

Alahverdian: "Being an American-based programmer, my obvious answer is no. Someone should not consider doing this. For the business owner, it's partly a personal decision, as well as a financial decision. In my opinion, outsourcing website design work that will be the centerpiece of your online business is a huge risk. I have seen really good websites created overseas, but also a lot of junk. The people you might wind up hiring will probably be minimum wage employees who simply don't care about your project. Thus, the quality is not going to be there. You'll also have to deal with language barriers, and in most cases, you have to deal with several middlemen."

Once a website is created and launched, are there less expensive ways to keep the site updated or make changes to the site, without having to use that same programmer and pay their hourly rate?

Alahverdian: "That's up to the business owner. They could invest the time necessary to learn basic HTML or DreamWeaver, for example, so they can make their own minor changes to the site. Depending on how the site is designed, there's also a program, called Contribute, from Adobe, that makes editing a website easy with no programming skills required. How easy it is to make changes to a site will come down to the knowledge and comfort level of the business owner, as well as how the website was initially created. There are ways to create websites that make it very easy for someone with no programming knowledge to later add or change products, text, or prices on their site, without using a website designer."

What are some of the elements that every e-commerce website must incorporate?

Alahverdian: "It's important to build online security into the site, especially if you'll be taking orders and having customers enter their personal data and credit card information. Your website designer should be extremely familiar with secure certificates. If you're building an e-commerce site, you also want that site to be a 'dynamic website,' and not just include static text and images.

"A dynamic website is one that uses a database to load your product and text for your website into a template file. Information, such as product pricing, gets entered into a separate database, from which the website pulls this data automatically and then displays it. This makes it easier to make basic changes to the site, plus helps ensure continuity in terms of placement of information, photos, and other content on each page of your site. ColdFusion is a main tool and server technology used to create dynamic websites.

"In terms of your product images, you want several versions of each image incorporated into the site. For example, there should be small, thumbnail images that load quickly. However, someone should be able to click on an image to see a larger, more detailed view of your product. Consumers want to see what they're buying, in detail. Quality product photos will definitely help to boost sales.

"A website should look professional and be very easy to navigate through, even for first-time visitors. People should be able to find exactly what they want in seconds, without having to look too hard or visit too many different pages within your site. The online ordering process also must be streamlined, so it's simple, fast, secure, and efficient. If you have five steps just to check out, this gives customers too many opportunities to leave your site without completing their order. It also adds to the confusion or frustration a visitor might experience.

"Your website should be efficient and in no way confusing to people. When it comes to website design, I consider myself a minimalist. I make sites look great, but I don't rely on fancy animations or other elements that will distract the site's visitors or simply provide eye-candy and take away from the overall objective. When used sparingly and correctly, animations can work well. They are overused way too often, however."

As a website is being designed, how much thought needs to be put into search engine optimization (SEO)?

Alahverdian: "Every website designer will know how to incorporate meta tags into a website properly. This is essential. Meta tags, however, can only do so much in terms of generating a prominent listing on the search engines. If search engine optimization is important to you, you'll need to carefully craft your text within the site to incorporate keywords, plus you'll want to hire a marketing company that specializes in SEO to help you. This, however, will cost you hundreds or thousands of dollars per month, because it's a timely process that requires expertise. SEO is not typically something a website designer will have the right expertise to do properly, so when you hire someone to handle this, make sure they have the experience and skills needed to do it right.

"What your website designer can do is create your site's meta tags, keep them up-to-date, and ensure that they're very specific to what you do. When a web designer adds text to your site, this should not necessarily be done in graphic form, because the search engines can't read text built into graphics or images as they catalog and rank your site."

How important is it for an e-commerce website to stay up-to-date with the latest web technologies?

Alahverdian: "It all depends on what you're doing. You don't need to have the newest and fanciest ways of doing things on your website, as long as it offers the functionality and visual appeal needed to achieve its objectives. Sometimes, the simplest way is the safest and best way, especially when you start having to deal with browser compatibility issues. If you use technologies or functions in your site that people have never seen before, you run the risk of confusing or scaring them, which could easily result in lost sales."

Do you have any other advice for first-time online business owners?

Alahverdian: "Focus on continuity when designing your website. For example, if you visit Amazon.com, the product descriptions, photos, buy icons, and other important elements are always in the same spot. The visitor never has to look around too much to find what they're looking for, because every product page is consistent in its format. The layout and color scheme of each page of your site should be consistent. Don't change text colors or fonts too much, for example. Make sure all of the text is visually easy to read, error-free, and well written. Again, your product photos also need to be clear and detailed."

In your opinion, what's the best way to find a competent website designer?

Alahverdian: "A word-of-mouth referral always works best. That's how I generate the majority of my business. You can also find highly qualified website designers by placing a free ad or responding to an ad on Craigslist.org. Before hiring someone, however, do your research and make sure they're capable of doing what you need to get done, that the designer is affordable, and that he or she is someone you'll be comfortable working with, potentially over the long-term."

Clay Baker
Founder, Clay Baker's Family Fishing
Website: www.ClayBaker.com

Unlike the other e-commerce business owners featured within this chapter, Clay Baker created the e-commerce aspect of his ClayBaker.com site after developing an interactive forum for fly-fishing enthusiasts that was initially established to be a fundraising and awareness boosting vehicle for several charitable organizations promoting the well-being and protection of the environment.

While Baker is an avid fly-fishing enthusiast, his full-time career involves working as a designer of high-performance "green" homes, through his business, Clay Baker Designs, LLC, which is based in Menlo Park, California. Because Baker works full time, for the past two years, ClayBaker.com has always been a secondary project, which he dedicates limited time to. Meanwhile, the site has grown dramatically in several different directions. So, within a year, he anticipates hiring at least one person to run the site on a full-time basis.

In this interview, not only does Baker discuss his experience running the e-commerce portion of his website, he explains the many benefits of providing information and an interactive forum that focuses on a specific topic (in this case fly fishing), in addition to the ability to buy products, within a single website.

How did you get started running an online business?

Baker: "I originally took a job with a software company out of college. I was involved with tech support and marketing. In 1995, I did a six-month stint working for Netscape Communications. At the time, version 1.0 of the Netscape web browser hadn't been released yet. Thus, over the years, I developed a decent background relating to work on the internet. While I didn't have technical expertise, I did have knowledge about website design and the internet before I launched ClayBaker.com. My college degree is in public relations.

"My goal was never to start an online business. It started out as an idea for a blog that never saw the light of day. The website was created, and the natural evolution of it was to add an e-commerce component. A few years ago, I was asked to visit Stamford University to speak to kids and their parents about green architecture. I design green homes as my full-time career. At the last minute, I changed the topic of my lecture from green architecture to involving people with fly fishing as a great way to teach them about the environment.

"The interest in this topic that people had lead me to create the Clay Baker.com website. I wanted to create an interactive forum, not just a blog. The primary focus of the site is to get people excited about the sport of fly fishing. Much like a fishing lodge, ClayBaker.com is a place where people can gather online to discuss something they enjoy. One of the newest elements added to the site is called MyStream, which is sort of like MySpace, but it's just about fly fishing.

"In addition to selling fly-fishing gear from other companies, we've created our own private-label products available exclusively on the site."

Once you developed the idea for the site, how long did it take you to get it online?

Baker: "Because I had a full-time job, I had little time to invest and no budget whatsoever. I intentionally decided to forgo writing a business plan. I didn't want to analyze this project to death. I believe too much analysis leads to paralysis. I specifically chose to do things very differently than I would have for a typical startup business. I wanted to see how far I could go on a shoestring budget, since this was never intended to be my full-time occupation.

"After developing the idea, I wrote out a detailed to-do list and gathered all of the tools I needed to launch the project. Because I had little time and no money, that narrowed down my choices in terms of technology. Thus, I needed to choose a hosted server and find a robust but inexpensive website design tool. Ultimately, I decided to use OSCommerce, which is an open source software application. It is totally free of charge. This was the perfect price, and the software offered plenty of flexibility. For me, OSCommerce was a slam-dunk. [See Chapter 6 for more information about OSCommerce, or visit www.oscommerce.org.]

"In one day, I downloaded OSCommerce and registered my domain name. Beyond that, I invested between 20 and 30 minutes per day, over a period of three months, to get the site launched and fully operational. Over the years, a lot of customized programming has been added to the site. From a functionality standpoint, it's equivalent to what companies pay hundreds of thousands of dollars for, but I have done it for a tiny fraction of that. I now have a website designer/engineer who helps me update and maintain the website.

"I took the Bowflex® approach to starting and operating this business. I work on it about 20 to 30 minutes per day, three to five times per week. From start to finish, working part time, someone can develop an active e-commerce website in under one week using OSCommerce."

Is there a significant learning curve to using OSCommerce?

Baker: "It's not as simple to use as they'd have you believe, but not so difficult that I couldn't figure out how to use it. What I chose to do was get the software set up, and then I tackled one problem at a time, as each appeared. The online user forums for OSCommerce offer a wealth of useful information and tutorials, which are totally free. I also found a handful of useful books about OSCommerce that were helpful. I found the books on Amazon.com, and a few of them are geared for non-programmers. Ultimately, using OSCommerce was the best decision I could have made for this site.

"I would recommend finding an OSCommerce guru to help you design and launch your site using this software. It will save you a lot of time and frustration, plus eliminate much of the learning curve. It's definitely a more productive way to move forward. I recommend leveraging the skills of other people as much as you possibly can. While now I can do the programming that's necessary, it's much more efficient to have someone who is an expert do it for me. I found my OSCommerce guru through Craigslist.org."

How did you decide what products to sell online?

Baker: "I don't look at ClayBaker.com as a business; however, because we're now generating revenues, the IRS does. The money that we make goes directly back into the website, or it gets donated to FishAid [http://claybaker.com/fishaid.php], which is an organization that raises money for groups that restore and protect natural habitats for fish.

"Instead of choosing what products to sell, many of them choose me. For example, St. Croix Fly Rods became excited about the educational component of what we're doing and made us the only online authorized dealer for their products, which until now have been sold exclusively through brick-and-mortar retailers.

"Once some of the products we began offering started to sell, I began looking for ways to generate more revenues, while also raising awareness for environmental issues. We ultimately created and began selling our own private-label lip balm, insect repellent, and sunblock products, which are all organic and chemical free. These products are sold exclusively through ClayBaker.com. They are great because they're profitable and people use them up and need to reorder again and again."

What was your biggest misconception about e-commerce before launching Clay Baker.com?

Baker: "I can't say I had any misconceptions, because I came into this with a lot of pre-existing knowledge about the internet and e-commerce. The biggest surprise for me, however, has been that so many people and companies have been eager to support the project and get behind it. For example, people from all over the world donated their professional-quality fly fishing photographs and artwork for use on the website. Thus far, in two years, ClayBaker.com has had more than one million visitors to the site from more than 80 different countries."

What challenges did you face getting the site up and running?

Baker: "Because I had a full-time job, dedicating the time necessary to launch this project was a challenge. It takes time keeping up with the daily tweaks to maintain the site. This is what led me to seek out help from a professional programmer. When I ran an ad on Craigslist.org looking for an OSCommerce guru, more than 100 people responded. I was looking for someone with very specific skills and experience to help me. As I was considering various people, I looked carefully at their portfolios of work and chose someone who had specific examples of similar work that they had done well in the past.

"One thing I discovered was that many people who pass themselves off as website designers know little about programming. They simply buy templates and then customize them for their clients. What I needed was someone with custom programming skills. Also, when hiring someone, choose someone who understands your server and knows what problems could occur there."

What advice do you have for someone first getting an online business started?

Baker: "More important than anything else, don't do it unless you're truly passionate about the project. The word 'passion' gets tossed around loosely. My acid test to measure my level of passion is to ask myself, 'If I don't do this, am I going to die?,' metaphorically, of course. If I don't feel that passionate about a project, I will walk away. Another thing to remember is that sheep die in herds, but the lone wolf always survives. So, if a lot of people are telling you not to do something, that could be a very good reason to do it. You should feel that your idea for an online business is so good, so unique, or so strong, that you absolutely must pursue it.

"The web today is all about finding greater interaction with people, in this case, your customers. Offering top-notch customer service and interacting with your customers is a time-consuming process, especially if you plan to do it well. When creating your site, find ways to promote interaction, not shy away from it, if you want to succeed."

In terms of advertising and marketing your website, what have you done that's worked particularly well?

Baker: "I have reached the conclusion that most advertising, like online banner advertising, is crap, when it comes to driving traffic to a website. It's like shooting a gun up into the air and hoping a duck falls. When I think about marketing and advertising, I focus on the three 'T's, which are 'target,' 'test,' and 'tweak.'

"Get to know who you customer is before you can even think about knowing the best places or ways to advertise. For my home design business, I only generate business through word-of-mouth referrals. I do no paid advertising at all. My only marketing materials for that business are business cards. My trick to deciding where to advertise is to figure out what my target customer is truly passionate about, and then I tap into that. My website is focused on someone's passion. We don't just sell fishing stuff.

"I spend just $50 per month using Google AdWords and have generated a really good level of ongoing traffic to the website. The best advertising that I do involves going out on the water and talking to other fisherman. Word-of-mouth advertising also works really well for ClayBaker.com.

"In terms of my private-label products, they are so inexpensive to make, I have had tremendous results giving away free samples to my target audience, as well as to fishing magazine writers and editors. This is a great way to create demand for a quality product."

Do you have any tips for setting up a merchant account?

Baker: "As an online business owner, you must accept major credit cards. This is not a choice. For someone first starting out, PayPal is a good solution, mainly because of the fraud protection program the company has in place. But ultimately, I'd recommend obtaining your own merchant account to accept credit cards, because this provides a more streamlined approach when it comes to a customer paying for their purchases online."

Do you have any other advice for an online business operator?

Baker: "Seek out the help you need from people who already have the expertise in specific areas. For example, if you need professional-quality product images for your site, hire a professional photographer. This will be a much better use of your time than going out, buying expensive photography equipment, and then learning how to take pictures. Likewise, if you need custom programming done, hire a programmer. Or, hire a professional writer to create the well-written text you need for your site. Your time is worth money. Don't waste it on tasks that other people could be doing for you in a more economical way. Focus on what you do best, but be knowledgeable about everything else that has to happen."

Kiel James Patrick

Founder, KielJamesPatrick.com

Website: www.KielJamesPatrick.com

At the age of 25, Cranston, Rhode Island-based Kiel James Patrick is an accomplished fashion model, having worked in the modeling and fashion industries since the age of 19. When in his early 20s, after rummaging through the attic of his parents' home and finding a chest chock full of his grandfather's old neck ties, he created a unique fashion accessory that involved cutting up the vintage fabrics and transforming them into ultra-trendy, hand-stitched bracelets that could be fashionably worn by males and females to complement any wardrobe style.

Patrick began wearing his creations every day while still in college and they quickly became a hit among his friends, all of whom wanted Patrick to create similar customized bracelets, using similar vintage fabrics.

Over a two-year period, Patrick fine-tuned his bracelets by adding a custom-designed, oversized signature button to clasp the bracelets around the wearer's wrist. He also added a custom-made liner fabric to his creations. Soon, the Kiel James Patrick (KJP) brand name was born.

Based on the demand among the people at Patrick's school for his bracelets, he soon decided to tap his entrepreneurial spirit, solicit the help of a few friends, and launch an online-based business to share his fashion accessory with the world.

Within weeks after launching and promoting his website, Patrick began receiving orders from high school and college students, as well as young adults from around the country. He also attracted the attention of fashion magazine editors, high-profile celebrities, and Hollywood stylists. This led to upscale boutiques expressing an interest in selling his unique products in their stores, although the main thrust of his sales continue to be generated from his custom-designed e-commerce website.

Because of the uniqueness of his fashion accessory products and the fact that he offers a variety of customizable options for each bracelet that's ordered (including the fabric style and the color button used), Patrick was unable to find an e-commerce turnkey solution to meet the needs of his online business, so he worked with a professional website designer to program and launch the KJP proprietary website.

Creating an e-commerce website from scratch allowed Patrick to incorporate a professional look that perfectly met his company's needs and image. By recruiting a friend, who is a skilled and experienced website designer, and making him a partner in the business, Patrick ultimately saved thousands of dollars in startup costs.

To help improve the site's content, Patrick also hired a professional writer to create much of the text and press materials used throughout the site, as well as a professional photographer to create the original product images.

Over the course of a year, while Patrick was establishing his brand and the business, he learned a lot about e-commerce and all of the business skills necessary to operate this type of venture.

While he admits that the time commitment has been significantly greater than he expected, the rewards have been well worth his time and financial investment as well as the sacrifices he's had to make in his social life to get the business off the ground.

In this interview Kiel James Patrick discusses his experience launching his product, his fashion brand, and his e-commerce website, plus offers valuable tips for entrepreneurs looking to follow in his footsteps.

What made you start the Kiel James Patrick brand and bracelet product line, and then decide to sell the products online using an e-commerce website?

Patrick: "I have always been interested in fashion. About six years ago, I was rummaging through a chest full of my grandfather's old neckties and admiring the different and unique vintage fabrics that were used to create men's fashions decades ago. The designs of the old fabrics captured my imagination. I began wearing the ties themselves, but one day decided to cut one of them up and sew it into a bracelet, which I began wearing to complement my preppy, New England style.

"On the very first day I wore one of the bracelets, the guys and girls at school started asking me where I bought the bracelet, because they wanted to buy them for themselves. For the next several months, I started making them for my friends and classmates. After about two years of making bracelets for friends and coworkers, I decided I could transform the idea into a business."

Once you decided to launch a business based around selling your one-of-a-kind hand-crafted bracelets, what steps did you take to bring the idea to fruition?

Patrick: "I knew I had created a very original fashion accessory product and for it to be successful, I needed to establish a unique and upscale brand through which to market the products. I wanted to create a brand that people would recognize outside of just the bracelets. One way I did this was to have over-sized, custom-made brass buttons created that showcased my brand name [Kiel James Patrick] and my company's logo. These buttons are used to fasten the bracelets around the wearer's wrist and add to the overall uniqueness of the product, while also helping to establish an identifiable brand.

"After having created my company name, logo, brand, and a unique product line, I quickly discovered this wasn't yet enough to obtain national retail distribution through upscale fashion boutiques. This is what led me to establish an e-commerce website. I wanted to reach the broadest audience possible, comprised of fashion-conscious high school and college students, as well as young adults.

"By creating a website, I began to build credibility for my company. One of my close friends is a highly skilled website designer, so I recruited him to help me launch the business. We started working day and night to get the website up and running. The site we created was done 100 percent from scratch. We opted to avoid using an e-commerce turnkey solution or any type of pre-created template, mainly because I needed very specific functionality from the site, plus I wanted my site to have a totally unique look. I didn't want other online businesses to easily be able to mimic the look of my site by using the same template.

"My website designer is a genius. He created a professional-looking website that is easy to customize and easy to navigate. I insisted that the whole website showcase the preppy, Martha's Vineyard type fashion and lifestyle that my company's products promote. Every element of the website, from the overall design and look, to the text and the product photographs had to remain totally consistent."

Once you decided to create your e-commerce website from scratch, what were some of the challenges you encountered putting the site together?

Patrick: "When you see one of the bracelets in person, they look great. One challenge was coming up with a consistent way to visually showcase the bracelets themselves, including the handcrafted stitching, the signature button, and the uniqueness of the vintage fabrics, using digital photographs to be displayed on the web. We needed to make our product photos look three-dimensional and extremely detailed, so they really emphasized the quality and uniqueness of the products. I hired a professional photographer to create the marketing pictures that involved models. For the close-up product photos, we bought an expensive, high-end digital camera, as well as a specialized light box, and took our own close-up product and fabric swatch shots. It took us a lot of time to get the products shots consistent and absolutely right for the website."

From a time investment standpoint, how long did it take from the time you decided to launch your e-commerce website to the time it went online?

Patrick: "I invested two years of hard work into the business itself, and about three months of work into the website design. This is in addition to the time the website designer invested to program the site. Now, I spend at least 30 to 50 hours per week running the business, but a lot of this time involves hand-crafting the bracelets themselves and handling the marketing for the website and the company.

"This has become a full-time job that consumes my life, but in a good way. I invest a lot of time communicating with customers via e-mail and over the phone to ensure my company offers the very highest level of customer service possible. To keep up with my orders, my friends and I are often up until 2 A.M. sewing the bracelets and fulfilling orders.

"One thing we added a few weeks after launching the website was a toll-free customer service phone number that customers can use to ask questions or place their order by phone. I think this helps to boost sales, and it definitely helps to enhance our company's credibility and the overall positive perception our customers and potential customers developed as they visit our website for the first time."

How much money did you initially invest to get your company launched?

Patrick: "My initial startup costs were around $15,000. However, if I had paid full price to have the website designed and the customized buttons manufactured, for example, my startup costs would have quadrupled."

Has anything unexpected happened since launching your business?

Patrick: "Yes. Many unexpected things have happened that have been both good and bad. Many people have approached us offering help or investment capital. I have invested a lot of time interacting with these people, only to discover they weren't legitimate or that they had an alternate agenda. On a more positive note, I've also become something of a celebrity among the junior high and high school girls who have purchased my bracelets. I have received some adorable e-mails from these customers who interact with me through the website, as well as through Facebook and MySpace.

"I'd have to say that the biggest misconception I had going into this whole online business was that my job would be basically done once the site went online. I figured customers would come flocking to the site and start placing orders, starting from day one. What I didn't realize is that to generate traffic to the site, a lot of additional time and money is needed, on an ongoing basis, to market the site and our products."

Initially, what did you do to drive traffic to your website?

Patrick: "Initially, to drive traffic to the website, we did grassroots marketing on Facebook and MySpace. I also supplied free bracelets to popular and trendy high school and college students who promised to wear and show off the bracelets at school and wherever they happened to be. This created a tremendous amount of positive word-of-mouth advertising, which translated into sales.

"We also focused our initial marketing budget on a comprehensive public relations campaign, which included sending product samples, press releases, and a professionally written company bio to a targeted list of over 100 fashion-oriented magazines, websites, and blogs, in hopes of generating free publicity. Through friends and industry connections, I also invested time to get my products onto the wrists of young celebrities, including actors and major recording artists. This too paid off in a big way, in terms of generating positive hype and demand for the products.

"Because our product is so unique, using Google AdWords or search engine marketing didn't really offer the tools we needed to promote the website properly, so we focused our energies elsewhere. For many types of online businesses, however, this type of advertising can really pay off and be cost effective."

[To read the actual press release and company background that was created and sent to the media to promote KielJamesPatrick.com, see Chapter 9.]

Looking back, are there any mistakes you made that you learned an important lesson from?

Patrick: "Actually yes. One mistake, if you want to call it that, was using my full name as the website's primary URL. My name, Kiel James Patrick, is both long and confusing for people to spell. I think this led to some problems for people trying to find our site. Right now, we're registering a handful of different domain names that are easier to remember and spell, such as KJPBrand.com. We'll then do some market research to determine which ones are best to promote in order to make it even easier for potential customers to find us on the web.

"Another mistake was initially trusting too many people who turned out to be dishonest. In terms of the website's design, we also wound up fine-tuning our online checkout procedure and eliminated several steps. We discovered we needed to make this process as streamlined, straightforward, and as fast as possible for the customer. Once our product pages sold the product, the customer needed to be able to click the mouse and quickly buy the product without the site giving them a chance to change their minds or get frustrated going through too many check out steps.

"Another mistake I made was hiring a graphic artist to design our company logo and other assets. He wound up charging us an outrageous amount of money to make changes to the designs and create something we actually wanted to use. Ultimately, it was our website designer who wound up taking on a lot of the tasks we had hired the graphic artist to handle. Before hiring a freelance expert of any kind, do your homework so you know exactly what you'll be paying for, and agree in advance to all of the terms, deadlines, and expectations."

Displayed boldly on the homepage of your website is a statement that announces you offer free shipping on all orders. How useful has this been as a marketing tactic?

Patrick: "We quickly discovered that by offering free shipping, it promoted sales. If you think your product is worth $25, jack up the price to $30 and offer free shipping. This allows you to promote something that's offered for free online, and customers love that. Nobody likes seeing the grand total listed on the shopping cart change once shipping and handling charges are added. We have received very favorable feedback as a result of offering free shipping. We boldly promote this throughout the site, including on the homepage and within the shopping cart/checkout page."

Because your products are custom-made, how do you handle product returns?

Patrick: "We would gladly replace an item that is improperly made, although this has never happened. However, our return policy, which is displayed prominently on the website, states that because each order is custom-made, we can't accept returns. The product that's displayed on our website's screen is exactly what the customer will get. Plus, we offer an easy-to-use sizing chart. This eliminates a lot of potential problems for the customer in terms of placing their order correctly.

"It is essential that an e-commerce business owner describe in detail what their company's policies are, including their product guarantees, warrantees, and return policy. In addition to describing our policies, we also stress that if anyone is unhappy with their product, for any reason, they should contact us so that we can resolve the problem. This gives us some leeway, when necessary, to bend the rules a bit instead of strictly adhering to our posted policies.

"While we state we will ship all orders within 48 hours, we also stress that due to unpredictable shipping times through the U.S. post office, it could take up to ten days for someone to actually receive their order. We do our best to set realistic expectations for our customers. In reality, we almost always ship orders within 24 hours to speed up the process and to keep our customers happy."

One of the steps involved with launching your business was to obtain a credit card merchant account. What process did you use to obtain this?

Patrick: "We shopped around for the best deal. However, my website designer has used a merchant account provider in the past for other projects and was very happy with them, so that's the company we ultimately went with. I wholeheartedly believe in pursuing personal recommendations or referrals whenever possible. This philosophy has saved me a lot of time, money, and frustration. Ultimately, the merchant account provider we selected had a very low startup fee, plus very competitive ongoing rates and fees.

"At this point, we accept credit cards or debit cards with the Visa or MasterCard logo. If we opted to accept American Express or Discover, it would cost us extra, so we decided it wasn't worth it. In terms of online payment options for our customers, we recently added Google Checkout functionality to our site. This speeds up the checkout time and streamlines the sales process for those who want to take advantage of the option."

In general, what would you say is the most important business skill someone needs to operate a successful e-commerce website?

Patrick: "Without a doubt, the most important thing to have is organizational skills! There are a lot of details and tasks you'll constantly need to be juggling and if you're not totally organized, important details fall through the cracks. For every aspect of the business, you have to have a system set up. Whether it's the manufacturing process, order processing process, bookkeeping tasks, or shipping, you need to have established methods for handling everything and then stick to those proven methods in order to stay organized and efficient. Otherwise, you start making costly and time-consuming mistakes.

"In terms of bookkeeping and accounting, I am working with an accountant whom I meet up with on a regular basis to make sure we're handling all of the financial aspects of the business correctly. I also meet periodically with our attorney to make sure we're handling the legal aspects of the business appropriately."

What advice do you have for someone first launching their own e-commerce business?

Patrick: "First, find someone who has already done this successfully in the past and who is willing to mentor you. Having someone available to answer your questions and provide reliable advice is extremely valuable. Second, develop a detailed and comprehensive business plan as one of the very first things you do.

"Without a business plan, it's way too easy to throw away your money on unimportant things, and then you'll be wondering what happened and why the money you need for important things isn't available. When I first started this business, a lot of my money wound up being spent on the wrong things, mainly because I lacked knowledge and a truly defined plan. I can't overemphasize the need for a well-written and thought-out business plan.

"When you launch your own business, you will encounter setbacks and frustrations. However, once everything is up and running, there is no better feeling than working for yourself and knowing that you have nobody to answer to but yourself. Operating your own business is truly a life-changing experience.

"Operating an online business is definitely not for everyone. Initially, you have to be willing to invest 80 hours per week into your venture, without earning a penny. Plus, you need to be willing to invest the right amount of startup capital needed to successfully launch your business. This often means putting your personal finances at risk and making many personal sacrifices. There are no easy paths to follow and no get-rich-quick schemes. The hard work you put in will put a strain on your personal relationships, but ultimately, it will all become worth it.

"Also, you need to start your own business, based on your own idea. You can't take an idea from someone else. You have to be passionate about the business you create and make it your own in every respect. Focus on starting *your* company, not *a* company."

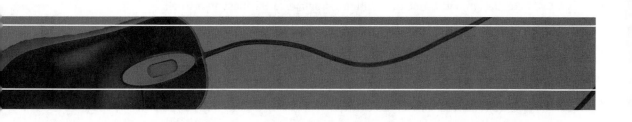

Glossary

*U*nderstanding the following terminology will help you better put all of the pieces together as you brainstorm, design, and launch your e-commerce website.

Advertising. A paid form of communication that allows you to market and promote your product to customers by conveying your exact marketing message. As the advertiser, you have total control over the message as well as where and when it appears or is heard. An online business can use many forms of media to advertise, including newspapers, magazines, radio, television, billboards, and newsletters, as well as online.

Affiliate marketing. Getting other online merchants and websites that are not direct competitors but appeal to your target market to promote your online business by displaying ads or offering links to your site on their site. In exchange, you pay that site either on a per-view or per-click basis, or offer a commission on any sales that site helps you generate through referrals.

Brick-and-mortar retail store. Any traditional retail establishment you'd typically find along Main Street in your neighborhood or in a local shopping center or mall. It can be operated by a local proprietor or be part of a nationwide retail chain.

Business plan. A detailed written document a businessperson creates when first brainstorming an idea for a new business venture and trying to determine whether the idea is feasible. A business plan includes financial projections and forecasts, as well as a detailed description of the business's goals, strategies, operational procedures, policies, and potential.

Catalog page. The part of an e-commerce website that showcases the specific products being sold. A catalog page can display one or more products at a time, and uses text, photos, graphics, animation, audio, or other multimedia elements to help sell each product.

Content. The combination of text, graphics, photographs, animations, audio, and other multimedia elements (also called assets) used to populate and create a website.

Conversion rate. The percentage of people who actually make a purchase from your website, compared to the number of people who simply visit. As an online businessperson, your goal is to create the highest possible conversion rate among your site's visitors.

Cost-per-click (CPC). How much it ultimately costs for each individual web surfer to click on an online ad for a website in order to visit that site. Some online ads are paid for based on the number of people who view them (impressions), while others are paid for based on the number of people who actually click on the ad.

Distributor. An authorized representative of a product manufacturer that sells large quantities of a specific product to retailers, who then sell them in much smaller quantities to consumers. As an online businessperson, you'll typically buy your inventory directly from manufacturers, distributors, importers (if the product is coming from overseas), or wholesalers.

Domain name registrar. The online services, such as GoDaddy.com and NetworkSolutions.com where someone can register a website's domain name.

e-Commerce turnkey solution. A complete set of website design and management tools that allows anyone to create, publish, and manage an e-commerce website for a set (often recurring) fee. These solutions require absolutely no programming knowledge. A computer with access to the internet is required to use them because the majority of these tools are online.

e-Commerce website. A website designed to sell products online. This type of website must quickly and accurately convey details about the product being sold and have a shopping cart feature that allows customers (web surfers) to safely and securely place their orders using a major credit card or other online payment method.

Google checkout. A service of Google, this is a way for e-commerce website operators to quickly and securely accept and process online payments.

Hit. Equivalent to one visitor to a website or one person viewing a specific webpage.

Homepage. The main page of any website where web surfers land when they enter a website's URL into their browser software.

HTML. HyperText Markup Language. A popular programming language used to create web pages, online documents, and websites. HTML defines the structure and layout of a webpage and allows for the use of hyperlinks.

Inventory. The amount or quantity of a specific product on hand (in your warehouse, for example) to sell to your customers.

Logo. A graphical image that establishes a visual icon to represent a company. A logo can also make use of a specific or custom-designed font or type style to spell out a company's name.

Mass-market retailer. Large retail superstores such as Wal-Mart and Target that cater to the mass market and carry a wide range of products.

Merchant. Someone who sells products or services. In terms of this book, it refers to someone selling products online using an e-commerce website.

Merchant account. Offered by a merchant account provider, such as a bank or financial institution, it is what's required for a business to be able to accept credit card payments. The merchant is charged various fees for the ability to accept credit cards from customers.

Meta tag. Specific lines of HTML programming within a website that are used to categorize a site's content appropriately in the various search engines and web directories. In addition to the site's description, title, and list of relevant keywords, you'll need to incorporate within the HTML programming of your site, a text-based, one-line *description* of the site (which again utilizes keywords to describe the site's content). A meta tag must be placed in a specific area of your page's overall HTML programming.

Niche market. A narrowly defined group of people who make up a target market. The people in a niche market (or target audience) can be defined by age, sex, income, occupation, height, weight, religion, geographic area, interests, and/or any number of other criteria.

PayPal express checkout. A service of PayPal, that allows e-commerce websites to quickly and securely accept and process online payments.

Product. The specific item or items an online business owner is selling.

Pubic relations. A marketing strategy used to obtain free editorial coverage in the form of product reviews, interviews, and/or product mentions in the media.

Retail price. The price a merchant (online or off) sells a specific product to their customers for.

Search engine. An online service that web surfers use to find what they're looking for on the web. A search engine is a comprehensive and ever-growing listing or directory of websites and their content.

Search engine marketing. Also referred to as *keyword advertising*. It involves paid keyword (text-based) advertising using Yahoo Search Engine Marketing,

Google AdWords, and/or Microsoft AdCenter. It drives very targeted traffic to a site easily and inexpensively. These short, text-only ads are keyword-based and appear when a potential customer enters a specific search phrase into a search engine.

Search engine optimization (SEO). Getting your site listed with the major search engines like Yahoo! and Google and then working to constantly maintain and improve your ranking/positioning with each so your site is easy to find and receives top placement.

Shopping cart. The module of an e-commerce website that serves as an interactive order form. It allows customers to input their order, shipping details, and credit card/payment information in a secure manner and then place their order electronically.

SSL (Secure Sockets Layer) encryption. The technology that allows safe and secure online credit card transactions (payments) via the internet. Proper encryption helps to prevent hackers from obtaining customers' credit card data and personal information, which could then be used to commit fraud or other crimes.

Target audience. The core group of people your business's products most appeal to and who comprise your core customer base.

Traffic. The number of web surfers who visit your site on an hourly, daily, weekly, monthly, or annual basis. A visitor is someone who surfs over to your website to explore. Your goal as an online merchant is to transform web surfers into paying customers who ultimately place orders for your product electronically when visiting your site.

URL (Uniform Resource Locators). A website address. A typical URL has three main components. The first part typically begins with www. or http://www. The second part of a URL is what you must select. The third part of a URL is its extension, typically .com. A variety of other extensions are available, such as .edu, .org, .net., gov, .info, .TV, .biz, .name, and .us.

Web browser. The software used by web surfers to surf the web. Microsoft Explorer, Safari, and FireFox are examples of popular web browsers. When creating an online business, it's essential that your website be compatible with all of the popular browsers.

Website template. Offered by e-commerce turnkey solutions providers. These are web page or overall website designs created by professional designers, artists, and/or programmers that can be fully customized to create a unique website.

Wholesale price. The discounted price you, the merchant, pay to purchase products in quantity from a wholesaler or distributor. Once products are acquired for resale, you then mark up the price and sell them to your customers at each product's retail price. Part of your profit is calculated based on the difference between the wholesale price of a product and the price you sell the product for. All of your other business operating expenses, however, must also be taken into account.

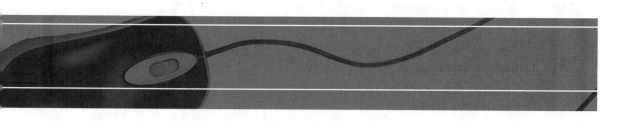

Index

Additional Books Written by Jason R. Rich and Published by Entrepreneur Press

The following books are now or will soon be available wherever books are sold, or can be ordered from the EntrepreneurPress.com website. For more information about these and other books written by bestselling author Jason R. Rich, visit his website at www.JasonRich.com.

Smart Debt

Entrepreneur Magazine's Personal Finance Pocket Guides

Buying or Leasing a Car: Without Being Taken for a Ride

Dirty Little Secrets: What The Credit Bureaus Won't Tell You

Get That Raise!

Mortgages & Refinancing: Get The Best Rates

Mutual Funds: A Quick Start Guide

Why Rent? Own Your Dream Home

Entrepreneur Magazine's Business Traveler Series

Entrepreneur Magazine's Business Traveler Guide to Chicago

Entrepreneur Magazine's Business Traveler Guide to Las Vegas

Entrepreneur Magazine's Business Traveler Guide to Los Angeles

Entrepreneur Magazine's Business Traveler Guide to New York City

Entrepreneur Magazine's Business Traveler Guide to Orlando

Entrepreneur Magazine's Business Traveler Guide to Washington, DC